EARLY CHILDHOOD ED

Sharon Ryan, ∟

For a list of other titles in this series, visit www.tcpress.com

(continued)

Standing Up for Something Every Day

Ethics and Justice in Early Childhood Classrooms

Beatrice S. Fennimore

Foreword by Celia Genishi

TEACHERS COLLEGE PRESS

Teachers College, Columbia University
New York and London

Published by Teachers College Press, 1234 Amsterdam Avenue, New York, NY 10027

Copyright © 2014 by Teachers College, Columbia University

Library of Congress Cataloging-in-Publication Data can be found at www.loc.gov.

ISBN 978-0-8077-5560-0 (paper)
eISBN 978-0-8077-7290-4 (ebook)

Printed on acid-free paper
Manufactured in the United States of America

21 20 19 18 17 16 15 14   8 7 6 5 4 3 2 1

This book is dedicated with deepest gratitude to the memory of Dr. Leslie R. Williams—brilliant professor, generous mentor, insightful guide, beloved friend, and enduring inspiration.

Contents

Foreword

Standing Up for Something Every Day—what a perfect title for a book that Beatrice S. Fennimore has filled with invitations to act on behalf of young children. As a prelude to these invitations, she raises the seemingly simple question that is at the heart of the book:

How do we advocate effectively?

Fennimore's answers to the question are many, complex, and detailed, yet highly accessible to a broad audience. I think that we as readers gain access to the complexity by looking through two lenses, one that is wide enough to take in large institutions and communities where individuals or groups engage in *advocacy* for children through familiar routes—for example, by writing letters, signing petitions, or participating in group protests. More often, however, Fennimore invites us to look through a fine-grained lens that focuses on the intimate communities of early childhood classrooms where individual teachers may choose to stand up for something every day. In small but important ways they address the book's subtitle: *Ethics and Justice in Early Childhood Classrooms.*

Thus in addition to advocacy on the macro-level, we are invited to consider the details of advocacy on the level of individual acts, which build on concerns for *ethics* and *justice,* as well as *respect for diversity.* Advocacy, ethics, justice, and respect for diversity—I repeat these words because they are what ground this work. They are concepts that are at the same time admirable, well worn but vital, abstract, and aspirational. Since they are terms with multiple meanings, Fennimore places them in relevant contexts and defines them carefully and clearly. With her deep experience as a teacher, teacher educator, parent, and advocate for children, Fennimore brings these key abstractions to earth by introducing us to four hypothetical "teacher-guides" named Aanetra, Emilio, Kira, and Jordan, who are composites of professionals that the author has known and worked with over the years. Each of them is committed to advocating through their actions—actions that are individual or collective, sometimes allied with children. It is not my role in a foreword to spell out intriguing details, but you may want a sense of the teacher-guides' approaches to advocacy. One example: Building on Fennimore's foundational principle that the language we use every minute of every day has a far-reaching impact, the four teacher-guides identify as problematic parents' or teachers' use of negative language about children who (1) have special needs, (2) live in public housing, (3) speak a language other than English, and (4) live in rural/agricultural areas. Each teacher-guide's intentions, plans, and actions are then concisely summarized. It is this kind of detail that moves us from aspirations to thinking concretely about possible solutions. Included in the details are widely available professional resources, such as the code of ethics of the National Association for the Education of Young Children (NAEYC), which are intended to help us construct our own solutions.

Accessibility, conceptual depth, and action-oriented details that link us to real-life early childhood settings are three characteristics that draw us to this book. Equally notable are its optimism and generativity. Fennimore laments early on that countries like the United States have done too little to address inequality and injustices in society and its schools, incorporating, for instance, the fact that the United States has done so little to reduce the number of children who live in poverty. This kind of knowledge can lead to understandable cynicism about the status of policies regarding children and families, but cynicism does not move us forward if our purpose is to be effective advocates. Thus Fennimore's realism is far outweighed by her optimism. Indeed her strong and reasoned optimism characteristically underlies her ideas and moves us to engage with the goals and recommendations she articulates.

As we readers choose to take thoughtful action in small steps with an optimistic spirit we will ultimately demonstrate that the ideas and practices specified here are generative: They take us somewhere over time; they "have legs." In short, this is a book for *all* who are committed to improving early care and education from the ground up. It is not just for those who already call themselves advocates, but is especially for teachers who may be encouraged through these pages to engage, question, reflect, and act, patiently taking small steps with the resources and support that Fennimore clearly offers. This is a book that informs us about advocacy on many levels, and, most important, it invites and inspires us to stand up and act.

—Celia Genishi, professor emerita,
Teachers College, Columbia University

Acknowledgments

It is impossible to write a book without the assistance of countless others—teachers, colleagues, friends, authors, reviewers, and family members who provide inspiration, encouragement, and support. Although space does not allow me to name them all here, my gratitude is most sincere.

Marie Ellen Larcada, senior acquisitions editor at Teachers College Press, has provided consistent and gracious support for this endeavor. Her wise counsel and ongoing encouragement have been deeply appreciated. Sharon Ryan, series editor, generously shared keen and candid insights that helped shape this book in meaningful ways. Celia Genishi has been a wonderful source of invaluable wisdom and kind encouragement for many years; she is a marvelous friend as well as a treasured professional colleague. I am deeply appreciative of her willingness to contribute the foreword to this book.

My wonderful husband Marvin Fein never ceases to amaze; he is a man of great kindness and indefatigable support. He is always willing to read my work with great care, and his thoughtful insights and suggestions are invaluable. My now grown daughters Sharon and Maryann continue to inspire and encourage me, and my darling grandchildren Nicholas, Josephine, and Tobias remind me continually of the unquestionable importance of standing up for children every day. I look back frequently on beloved family members and teachers whose lives touched me deeply; my awareness of, and gratitude for, their powerful influence deepens daily.

Thanks to Ysaaca Axelrod, who provided me with early guidance on the development of my hypothetical teacher-guide Emilio and translated some of his thoughts and words into Spanish. Thanks also to my graduate assistants LaNa Howard and Tanisha L. Wilkes, who read and commented carefully on drafts of the chapters. I also appreciate the time that Emily Levine gave to reading the manuscript and sharing her insights. I owe oceans of gratitude to Rosie Gundy for her cheerful and outstanding assistance in editing and preparing the book manuscript.

Almost 30 years ago, I sat in the cafeteria of Teachers College, Columbia University, with Leslie Williams, my wonderful professor and chair of my soon-to-be-completed dissertation. She told me that it was time to start thinking about my future career and to set my sights on new challenges. Leslie recently had become editor of the Early Childhood Education Series for Teachers College Press, and on that day she invited me to submit a proposal for my first book—*Child Advocacy for Early Childhood Educators*. I was momentarily speechless at the offer, but then quickly said yes. I had already learned that an invitation from Leslie was never to be taken lightly. She had a gift for opening the right door and guiding you through it. Leslie's untimely death from cancer in 2007 left so many of us to miss her so much. It is more than fitting that this book is dedicated to her treasured and enduring memory.

Introduction

I took my first university course in child advocacy as a doctoral student in the early 1980s. It was a one-time colloquium taught by a recent graduate of my program at Teachers College, Columbia University. She had received a prestigious fellowship and soon would be leaving New York City. I was so fascinated by the course topic that I approached the instructor in the cafeteria one day toward the end of the course to ask how I might seek greater involvement in child advocacy. She startled me by quickly suggesting that I take her place as an adjunct instructor at a small private college in Manhattan, where she had been teaching an undergraduate course in child advocacy during her doctoral studies. When I told her that I did not feel that I had a sufficient knowledge base to do this, she said, "I have not been able to find anyone who feels that they know enough to teach this course. I promised the college a replacement and I'm running out of time. I suggest that you make the most of this opportunity and undertake a significant independent study as you teach."

Taking her advice with considerable trepidation, I began, with my very first college class, to explore the incredibly complex challenges facing children in America. My students and I shared alarm and concern about the information we were reading about unregulated child care, child maltreatment, fiscal improprieties in the foster care system, and multiple dilemmas and inequities related to the experience of child poverty. As we became more aware of the disturbing evidence that children in America were not faring well, we wondered why this situation was not more visible as a national concern. One of my students asked, "Can we at least take some comfort in knowing that people are caring and trying to do something about this?" I answered in the affirmative, because I was increasingly aware of all the advocates who were working diligently to bring these issues to public light. My assumption was that, once people in the United States were aware of the urgent needs of children, they would act.

OUR NATION KNOWS BUT DOES NOT ACT

However, about 10 years later, Dr. T. Berry Brazelton (1990), America's pre-eminent pediatric scholar and practitioner, wrote an article in the

New York Times Magazine titled "Why Is America Failing Its Children?" In that article he discussed the significant problems that were affecting our national child population. As a member of the then-formed National Commission on Children, he indicated that he had once believed that Americans appeared not to care because they did not know what was happening to children in their nation. Sadly, he had since changed his mind. Americans in 1990 did know but continued not to care—our nation, as he described it, apparently had become numb to the hopelessness of so many of our children.

Mary Cunningham (1990), former director for the National Commission of the International Year of the Child in 1971, wrote a letter to the *Times* in response to the Brazelton article. "Brazelton should know," she wrote, "that such commissions are appointed as a palliative, a substitute for taking action. This is the third national commission appointed in 10 years . . . while the resumes of commission members may be enhanced by such appointments, the recommendations for changing children's lives fall on deaf ears" (p. 1).

In the many subsequent years that I have continued to be a teacher educator, author, and advocate for children, I have constantly reflected on the problems raised by both Brazelton and Cunningham early in my career. How do we influence communities as well as a nation to act in a way that creates compassionate care about social neglect, inequality, and suffering in the lives of children? How can we take the results of high-profile commissions on children "to the ground," where activists often struggle without resources or recognition to create real change for children? How might we support the courage of people who are speaking out against oppression without prestigious universities or politically powerful communities to back them up? And, central to the purpose for this book, how do classroom teachers, whose important work is so central to the well-being of children, become visible and respected advocates for the children in their own classrooms?

GETTING CLOSER TO THE FIRE

In their book *What's Worth Fighting for Out There?* authors Michael Fullan and Andy Hargreaves (1998) urge all educators who want to make a difference to get closer to the fire; that is, get closer to the real problems that contain both risk and genuine possibility for change. Teachers, of course, are on the front line of "the fire" as they work every day with children whose lives reflect the inconsistencies of a society that claims to care about them while neglecting or oppressing them. Teachers are not just caring professionals—they are the potential change makers "on the ground" whose activism can bring democratic ideals to life.

Teacher educators—those in the academy who prepare future teachers through coursework and supervision of field experience—also have the opportunity to get closer to the fire. Teachers and teacher educators may experience "the fire" in different ways, but we all have the opportunity to see and speak out about what is *really* happening to children in school and society. Thus, I believe we have the responsibility to collaborate carefully with one another, to recognize what is unfair and unjust in the lives of children, to extend compassion and care to all children, and to be courageous in bringing child-related injustices and inequalities to public light.

The fire exists in many places in our lives as educators—continued school segregation, child poverty and all its ramifications, unequal school resources, serious problems encountered by families and communities, inappropriate pressures of standardized testing, ethical violations, deficit-based and denigrating talk about children with certain attributes or labels, and unkind or even harsh treatment of vulnerable young children whose lives are the hardest and who need our help the most.

The fire also exists in our daily lives in the classroom and the countless daily decisions we make as early childhood educators. We know we approach our young students with deeply held beliefs and a wide array of personal experiences that will structure our thought process in the classroom. There are many different ways to respond to children who are poor, disabled, born to undocumented parents, living with gay or lesbian parents, or sullen and withdrawn in school. These can extend from acceptance and encouragement to harmful deficit-based disparagement or worse. Ultimately, the ways in which we *do* respond will increase or decrease the equity and justice our students experience in our classrooms. Early childhood educators who want to be powerful advocates must do the careful reflective thinking that creates an intentional and purposeful approach to teaching young children in America—a nation that still seems not to care about many of its young.

STANDING UP FOR SOMETHING EVERY DAY

This book is written for you, the present or future teacher in the early childhood classroom, who wants to make a real difference in the lives of children. It will focus on your daily life as a teacher and the ways in which it can be shaped by your belief system and your commitments as well as your actions. Every day, early childhood educators encounter situations that require a caring and ethical response. Our commitment to fair treatment of children and our respect for diversity must always be evident in our schools, programs, and classrooms.

While the main focus of this book will be on the ways in which your intentions as a teacher will affect your life with your students in the classroom, it will not stop there. I am making the assumption that your classroom life will affect and be affected by your relationship with your administrators and colleagues, your interactions with parents and families, and ultimately your sense of responsibility to your community and society. Thus, when I say classroom life, I ultimately mean the totality of your experience as an early childhood educator. All of your professionally based relationships and interrelationships will influence the ways in which you conduct life in your classroom. Likewise, the way you conduct your life in your classroom will in some way affect all others with whom you come into contact as a teacher.

It is not easy to know what to do. Let's take a minute to consider three hypothetical, everyday dilemmas:

You take the children in your kindergarten class to a local playground. Many of them are climbing and sliding on equipment when a child with a significant physical disability and her caregiver approach the slide. Some of your students stare and move away; one student says, "You can't play here!"

Some of the children who attend your rural Head Start program live in trailers in more remote areas and do not have running water. You have heard some teachers calling them "trailer kids." One teacher at a faculty meeting says, "I wish these parents would care enough to keep their kids clean."

You teach in a child-care center serving an impoverished community. Many of the children, as well as a number of employees, depend on the daily hot lunch served at community tables at the center as their main meal of the day. At your table, several employees warn the children not to put more on their plates than they can eat. You are concerned that this seems to intimidate the children and you are not sure they are getting enough to eat.

We would anticipate that there could be many different ideas about the appropriate and most helpful response to the above situations. However, there is no doubt that each situation does require reflection and action. We all struggle to some degree when called on the spot to respond to complex and difficult circumstances. Is it really our responsibility to take the risks involved in taking a stand? It can be easier to think, "Why bother when saying something isn't going to change anyone's mind," or, "I have too much to do already to get involved in other people's problems," or, "I don't want to get myself into a situation where people might get angry and retaliate." Such thoughts can block our sense of professional efficacy—our belief that we have the power and responsibility to protect children through our words and actions.

As a present or future teacher you have enormous real-world power to reach directly into the lives of children and change them for the better. "There is no other profession in the world that directly or indirectly touches the lives of people at the same level as teachers do" (Boutte, 2008, p. 166). This power, your power, should be recognized and acted upon every day.

TAKING A STAND: PERSONAL, PROFESSIONAL, AND POLITICAL

I believe there are three different dimensions of taking a stand for children. Every response to unfairness or injustice is *personal*, because it reflects our emotions and beliefs. However, because we are responding to situations within our employment responsibilities, our *professional* identities (and professional ethics) also are involved. Finally, our responses are *political* because the rights and responsibilities inherent in a just resolution of unfairness or discrimination are ultimately established in society by governments. Let's take a brief closer look at each of these dimensions.

The Personal

Actions that reflect what we say we believe are powerful; children and adults do know when they are in the company of those who consistently act on their commitments to fairness. Some might refer to this as "walking the talk"—holding oneself responsible for actually demonstrating the values that one claims to hold and expect from others. This kind of integrity and authenticity can never be taken for granted. Rather, it is a dynamic life's work that changes from young adulthood through all of the stages of maturation and age. In each phase of our careers, especially when we are discouraged by the roadblocks to our ideals, we must visibly retain the integrity of our stated intentions. The personal is central to the professional—the desire to follow the path of justice and fairness guides us to do the best we can in every way, every day, for the children we teach.

The Professional

As early childhood educators, we belong to a great profession with a distinguished history. When we are in the classrooms of our schools or programs, we are expected to embody best practices as well as our code of professional ethics. The parents and caring adults who entrust us with their children believe that we will treat them with great care and kindness. We must honor that trust by putting the children first. This means that we must never lose sight of their need to experience healthy growth and a sense of well-being in safe and compassionate environments. Where questions may exist about practice, we consult our code of professional ethics in collaboration with colleagues and administrators to make strong and informed decisions.

As professionals, we need to uphold and support our colleagues as well as the children. The importance of being helpful and agreeable, however, must be balanced with the importance of being ethical. The development of professionalism is also a life's work—complex, but well worth the effort for all involved.

The Political

Some might be surprised to see the word *political* applied to early childhood education. However, concepts of justice, ethics, and diversity are embedded in the political as well as the professional and personal. It is essential to see the connection between our commitment to fairness and the civil and human rights on which we all depend. I take exception in this book to those who indicate a belief that *social justice* is just a "liberal" (as opposed to "conservative") political interest or indeed that it should be viewed as a political choice at all in our democracy. My belief is that the constitutional protections of liberty and equality should be viewed as both a civil right and a civic responsibility by every American. Thus, social justice as it relates to rights cannot be pigeon-holed into terms like "conservative," "liberal," "Left," and "Right." Our Pledge of Allegiance includes the words, ". . . with liberty and justice for all." That stated commitment to justice transcends political parties and preferences.

CONCEPTUAL FRAMEWORK AND THEORETICAL TOUCHSTONES

The framework of this book might be visualized as a large tent held up with three sturdy conceptual stakes. The tent is child advocacy, which I consider the fundamental act of standing up for children in the context of one's daily work. The "tent" of child advocacy is held firmly in place with three important concepts: *justice, ethics,* and *diversity.* I believe it is important for the field of early childhood education to take a refreshed look at the complex ways in which these concepts are interlinked and mutually essential to forward movement for children in this nation. A good place to start is the connection between the conceptual framework and the theoretical touchstones of this book.

The concepts of advocacy, justice, ethics, and diversity are embedded in several related theories. For example, the work of John Rawls in *A Theory of Justice* (1971) emphasizes justice as "the first virtue of social institutions" (p. 3). When Rawls (2001) revisited this seminal work before his death, he emphasized that justice was political in nature. Ultimately, he believed justice is a basic sense of fairness that should serve as a moral and political guide for all democratic institutions. Moving from the overarching insight of the work of Rawls, this book extends social justice into theories related to diversity, cultural power, privilege and oppression, ethical responsibility, and teacher talk.

The idea of "standing up for something every day" embraces the call of critical theorists to recognize not only the imbalance of power and opportunity in society, but the ways our conceptualization of "knowledge" and the process of schooling itself can privilege some while marginalizing others (Ryan & Grieshaber, 2004). For example, in what way might the current conceptualization of school readiness support existing social and economic stratifications? Is it likely to benefit children of privilege, who might come to school with more of the commonly held attributes of "readiness"? Is it likely to ignore or give lesser value to the different skills and attributes of children who live in poverty? Who has the power to create the "knowledge" of what all children must know at school entry in order to be successful, and how can that "knowledge" create automatic marginalization of some children and privileging of others as they all walk through the school door for the first time?

An answer to why we must stand up and act in response to unfairness and injustice comes from the theoretical work of Mikhail Bakhtin. In his work *Toward a Philosophy of the Act,* Bakhtin (1993) argues that we constantly are seeking uniqueness in dialogue with the world and that we can never retain neutrality toward the moral and ethical demands of which we become aware. He argues that every moment involves a choice of response for which we are responsible; we must not abdicate this responsibility (Pollard, 2011).

The collective action theory of Jurgen Habermas supports the idea that moral norms, such as those in educational institutions, must be arrived at through dialogue with others (Head, 2008). This gives critical importance to ethical examination of the ways in which teachers talk to one another about students in schools. Does our discourse construct or weaken the ethical environment for which we are responsible as educators? Pierre Bourdieu, in his book *Language and Symbolic Power* (1991), elaborates on language as the cultural power that can retain and reinforce structures of privilege, stratification, and discrimination in social institutions. While many people believe that "just talking" has little effect on others, John Austin emphasizes in his book *How to Do Things with Words* (1962) that language is a behavior that makes things happen and keep happening in certain ways. These theorists help us to understand the deep ethical dimensions of our use of labels and denigrating or deficit-based descriptions of children in our daily lives in schools.

All of these theoretical touchstones intersect and interact to provide windows of insight into diversity, ethics, justice, and the everyday lives of educators in early childhood classrooms.

STRUCTURE OF THE BOOK

This book is written to support a vision of what is possible in your classroom, and your full professional life, every day. This vision is idealistic, but is developed to help you focus on the *possible*. The book begins with a chapter on intentions and their role in helping you think about diversity, ethics, and justice in your classroom. In Chapter 2, the concepts of "teacher talk," and the power of descriptive language about children, are explored. The discussion of diversity in Chapter 3 may challenge you to think differently about diversity than you have in the past. The approach I have selected is one in which *all* people should see themselves as part of the diversity of the world in which they live. This is very different from establishing a norm (White, middle class) and then viewing those who differ from the norm as *diverse*. When teachers see themselves as part of diversity in human life they may be more likely to look beyond surface characteristics to see not only the differences in others but the similarities that build interconnectedness and interdependency. However, Chapter 3 also recognizes the forms of oppression, discrimination, privilege, and power that are experienced by different people in our society. This recognition relates closely to Chapter 4, which explores the dynamic and complex interplay of ethics and moral action in early childhood classrooms.

In Chapter 5, the concept of readiness is examined as an example of ways in which the critical application of advocacy, justice, ethics, and respect for diversity has an impact on life in the classroom. Then, in Chapter 6, we turn to an examination of the ways in which curriculum, projects, and interpersonal interventions help children in the classroom to learn and practice the concepts of fairness. Finally, in Chapter 7, we take a hopeful look at the ways in which the commitments of early childhood educators can influence their colleagues, schools, community, and a world greatly in need of a renewed sense of social justice for children and families.

Each chapter will end with suggestions for how to get started and questions for reflection and discussion. There also will be four hypothetical teacher-guides, introduced in Chapter 1, who provide complex and thoughtful approaches to implementing chapter ideas in their own early childhood settings.

PUTTING IT ALL TOGETHER: BEING THE CHANGE

Our diverse nation, like others around the globe, faces economic and political uncertainties. This adds to the frustration that early childhood educators feel about persistent child poverty combined with a lack of funding for high-quality educational programs. To complicate things further, we all inevitably encounter some people—parents, colleagues, administrators, or politicians—who seem to lack competence, efficacy, or integrity. Every person and professional who devotes her or his life to the betterment of others experiences discouragement at times. However, each and every one of us does have the choice, as Gandhi once indicated, of "being the change we want to see in the world." We can, on personal, professional, and political levels, seek to embody and model for others what we believe is right and just. This book is written to help you to *be the change*, and stand up for something, every single day. And that *something* is our children and their future shaped by an education that is based on justice, ethics, and deep respect for diversity and all of its social ramifications.

ONE

Teacher Intentions Hold the Key

Your intentions as a teacher will play a very important role throughout your career; ultimately they will define you as a professional. As you shape your intentions, ask yourself, "What do I want everyone with whom I have worked as a professional to remember about me at the end of my career?" Once you really know who you want to be and how you want to be known, you are on your way to constructing a very strong and powerful identity as a teacher.

This book is written to encourage you to build your career with intentions that are strongly focused on child advocacy, ethics, social justice, and respect for human diversity. I believe that these interlinked intentions will help you to rise above discouragement, stay committed, support the growth of every child in your care, and lead others by example. Most important, they will help you to fully meet the high calling of teaching—the call to be a principled and compassionate social leader whose enduring impact on children will reverberate throughout your school or program, and ultimately your society. Let's get started by thinking about what the above intentions look like in the classroom.

JUSTICE AND ETHICS THROUGH THE EYES OF A CHILD

Imagine that this is your first day of kindergarten at a new school. It is the middle of the school year, and you don't know anyone. Almost all of the children and adults in the school are speaking English. You know some English words, but not many. Your family speaks a different language at home. Right now you are confused about what is happening in the room because children are moving into different play areas. Your teacher smiles, says your name the same way your mother says it, and guides you to a corner with a lot of blocks. You feel shy with the other children but start to enjoy building a little block house by yourself.

Suddenly two other children in the block area walk over to you, laugh at what you are doing, and call you a name that you do not understand. Their faces do not look very nice. Frightened, you look up and see your teacher walking over very fast. She puts her hand on your shoulder and speaks calmly but firmly to the other children. Even though you cannot understand the words she is saying, you can see that the other children listen to her and then say something that seems much nicer to you. You continue to play with your blocks, feeling better about your day.

After everyone cleans up from play, the teacher reads a book with beautiful pictures about friends. You recognize the subject because you understand the word *friends* and also because there are many pictures of children helping one another. The book has some words in the language that you speak; this seems wonderful to you. There is a game after that, and the teacher shows all the children how to play the game with a partner. You do not need to know all the words for the game because you can follow your teacher, your partner, and the other children. Your teacher keeps smiling at you and helping your partner to show you what to do next. She even says good-bye to you in your own language! By the time you leave for home, you have started to be confident that school will be a place where you can feel comfortable with the teacher and the other children.

JUSTICE AND ETHICS THROUGH THE INTENTIONS OF A TEACHER

The above narrative, written through the eyes of a young child, is a simple one. It might appear to be just a description of "good teaching." However, the well-developed teacher intentions that it reflects are highly complex. This teacher is not merely being "nice" or "encouraging." Rather, she understands the social oppressions that find their way into classrooms of young children and is determined to take a stand against them. Her intention to interrupt discrimination and support fairness and equality is the structure of her planning and action in daily classroom life. Her intention is to implement what might be identified as *social justice teaching*—intense caring about the common good and purposeful opposition to ramifications of social and political forces that can harm vulnerable young children (Kohl, 2000).

Her focus is not only on the children whom she considers to be "different." Rather, she thinks it is very important that all the children in the room benefit from her insistence on fairness—she wants them all to learn to be good citizens in a democratic and caring classroom environment (Dombro, Jablon, & Stetson, 2011). This book is strongly aligned with the concept of social justice teaching through the lens of advocacy, ethics, social justice, and respect for diversity.

This early childhood teacher has a firm grasp on the intentions and actions necessary to work for social change in her own classroom. Through her approach to *every* child as a worthy person and capable learner, she demonstrates enacted regard for all her students (Williams, 1989). She finds support for her dynamic respect for human diversity not only in the ideal of justice within a democratic society, but in the fundamental ethical edict that "no child be harmed" in the process of education (National Association for the Education of Young Children, 2011).

Her students are so fortunate! They spend every day in a classroom with a teacher whose intentions support a fair and ethical learning community. As learners, as well as future citizens, they are benefitting from the daily intentions of their teacher. All children in America need teachers like this in their lives!

A VISION FOR YOUR OWN CLASSROOM

The teacher above, of course, is or can be you! This book is written to support the daily activation of your intentions to be an educator known for strong commitments and dedication to the optimal development of all children. The following section will discuss situations and social conditions that you will need to keep in mind as you develop your determination to remain strong in your dedication to be a powerful force in your classroom, school, and society.

The field of early childhood has long been guided by a vision of advocacy, justice, and ethics in the context of respect for diversity (Wollons, 1993). But what does that vision *mean* for real teachers in real classrooms? Some readers of this book may recall their first days in teacher preparation classes, when every idealistic word about teachers changing the world seemed to ring true. Why would we ever doubt our ability to be fair and ethical and to embrace the principles of social justice and respect for diversity? Shouldn't such intentions just come naturally to all teachers who dedicate their lives to children? Yes, one might argue, they should! But often in teaching what first appears to come naturally, ultimately may require a lot of reflection, determination, and hard work.

Once we complete our preparation as teachers and find ourselves employed with real children in actual classrooms, difficulty in retaining our ideals can surface quickly. Challenges with administrators, colleagues, and parents can begin to emerge. We may become aware of problems that exist in our schools and in the communities they serve. Children may seem at times to resist our efforts to support their learning and development. We can be discouraged by the reality of the impact of problems like adult addiction, family turmoil, or poverty on the daily lives of our students. Fairly soon, for many of us, there can be quite a long list of potential barriers to our retention and implementation of the ideals that we once formed so easily.

Added to possible frustrations might be the ways in which our work is perceived by others. Family members or friends might wonder aloud why someone with our talents would have selected a "low-status" career teaching young children. We might turn on the nightly news for a few relaxing minutes in front of the TV and find ourselves listening to a legislator who is blaming the very complex economic, social, and political problems of our nation on *teachers*. Possibly, we find that even modest living expenses seem to exceed our salaries, especially if we have a family to support. In fact, although we work very hard to care for other people's children, at the same time we might be having considerable trouble finding adequate and affordable child care for our own!

For the above reasons and many others, we face pressing questions about our power as early childhood educators—can we really hold on to our ideals and continue to believe that the important work we do is essential to the lives of many children and families? Moreover, can we really stand up for our beliefs about advocacy, diversity, ethics, and justice in ways that make a true difference in school and society? This book is written to say *yes*, we can do these things—not easily, but with insight, determination, persistence, and ideals that refuse to waver from their focus on the well-being of children in our classrooms and our nation.

THE PERSISTENT CHALLENGE OF CHILDHOOD IN THE UNITED STATES

Early childhood teachers confront some of the most complex and pressing social dilemmas of our nation every day. Young children come to their schools and programs reflecting the ramifications of problems such as family stress, poverty and unemployment, lack of access to medical and dental care, inadequate nutrition, child abuse, community violence, and commercialized media exposing them to games and toys that undermine healthy social and emotional development (Children's Defense Fund, 2011).

Today in America, we appear to be facing an escalating child crisis. As Linda Darling-Hammond (2012) recently indicated:

> We live in a nation that is on the verge of forgetting its children. The United States now has a far higher poverty rate for children than any other industrialized nation in the world . . . a more tattered safety net . . . and greater disparities in wealth than any other leading country. (p. vii)

It is going to take a lot of commitment and resilience for early childhood educators to retain vision in these difficult times. We need to continue to find ways to care about and act on behalf of children, especially when it seems that many in power do not.

FOCUSING ADVOCACY ON ALL CHILDREN IN THE UNITED STATES

Traditionally, child advocacy has focused on children in our society whose needs are not being met. It has been very important to focus on the children who are suffering the most from such adversities as poverty, institutional racism, and gross educational inequalities. However, in this book, I am going to suggest that advocates extend their articulated commitment to every child living in the United States today. Why? First of all, I would argue that every child is affected in a negative way by life in a society that allows some children to suffer so deeply and to lose their opportunities for optimal development. Why would children believe in the ideals of democracy when they are well aware of significant inequities experienced by some children—frequently including children who are obviously marginalized in their own schools? Also, the myopic social selfishness that allows shameful neglect of many children can interfere with the development of empathy, compassion, and commitment to community in any child. Including all children in our advocacy and concern may strengthen policy and advocacy initiatives. From a historical policy perspective, many years of advocacy, research, publications, conferences, summits, and national commissions have not been able to change the hearts and minds of the many in America who dismiss any sense of responsibility for the problems of "other people's children." Including all children may help to ameliorate this problem!

I want to clarify that I am *not* suggesting that we silence our voices of outrage focused on poverty, homelessness, persistent racism, early incarceration, and other incredibly serious dilemmas! But I do think it is time to speak out with concern about how the greed and inequality that exist in our society are affecting all children. My hope is that this might strengthen a sense of common cause—an urgent need for all people to create a new nation in which the safe and healthy development of all children is an irreducible priority.

Child Problems Are Pervasive

Many serious problems such as child suicide, depression, and addiction occur on all levels of society (Children's Defense Fund, 2011). In fact, recent research suggests that affluent suburban children experience substance abuse and depression at a higher rate than children who live in the inner city (Luthar & Barkin, 2012). Among other serious dilemmas that touch the lives of many American children across class lines are family violence, sudden parental unemployment, mental illness, and divorce (Fennimore, 2011). Clearly, there are many ways in which problems and challenges touch the lives of all our children.

Including broadly based child problems in our advocacy can push larger questions to the surface. How much support are we really giving to our child population in the United States? Are we protecting our child population from harmful influences? These and many other questions can lead to much-needed reflection on our national commitment to children and our need to prioritize them as a significant concern—even if they do not appear to be imminently in harm's way.

Social "Nastiness" and Consumerism: A Good Place to Start

I would suggest that a pervasive level of social nastiness and the constant manipulation of children for the economic gain of adults would be a good place to start an examination of America's child- and family-related values.

The problem of "nastiness." All children today are affected by what James Garbarino (1995) has termed the social toxicity and increasing "nastiness" that are commonplace in American life. Children may be experiencing this toxicity in schools through cruel actions and words of their peers—forms of bullying. However, they also may be observing and experiencing nastiness of the part of *adults* on a daily basis. This can include hostile words and actions while driving cars, speaking angrily on cell phones in public places, pushing or cutting lines in stores, or just generally treating others without personal regard or respect. Civility—constant awareness of others and intention to treat others in kind and ethical ways—appears to be lacking in many aspects of our adult society (Forni, 2002). Children follow the example of adults; therefore, it is time to talk about the effect of nastiness and a lack of adult civility on the development of all our children.

Consumerism and greed. Added to social toxicity and lack of civility in our society are the selfishness and greed reflected in a pervasive emphasis on consumerism. There is no escape from consumerist values in our media-saturated society; children are affected by them early in life. Linked to a focus on consumerism is vacuous adult behavior that prioritizes personal acquisition above moral values and respect for the rights and needs of others. A look at headlines on any given day tells us that adults, including some of the most successful and affluent, are losing their grip on ethics. Marian Wright Edelman, executive director of the Children's Defense Fund, makes an important point:

> What's wrong with our children?—Adults telling children to be honest while lying and cheating. Adults telling children not to be violent while marketing and glorifying violence. . . . I believe that adult hypocrisy is the biggest problem children face in America. (Shetterly, 2005, p. 3)

I would argue that the problems of greed and hypocrisy are contributing directly not only to a callous disregard for child and family poverty, but to the moral and emotional vacuum felt by many children whose economic needs are well met.

Children and consumerism. All American children are affected by the consumption-saturated world in which they live. Corporate investment in advertising to children has risen from $100,000 in 1983 to a current $17 billion annual expense (Levin, 2011). Children who are poor are constantly manipulated to desire toys and games that are completely out of their family's economic reach. Those who advertise are blind to the children's frustration and disappointment. However, even the children whose families can afford to continually meet their requests for purchases are negatively affected by consumerist advertising. Often they develop the perception that material possessions are the most important thing to seek in life and the best indicator of the quality of a person. This leads to a form of "affluenza" that prioritizes consumption over positive human qualities such as understanding, kindness, and fairness. The American Academy of Pediatrics considers "affluenza" ultimately to be a cause of adolescent depression and suicide (De Graaf, 2005).

All adults should take action. Our society as a whole must take a careful inward look at our standards of civility and our child- and family-related values. Moving as a nation from consumerism to humanism and compassion would wake us up to not only the unjust misery that so many children experience, but the damage that empty, selfish values and behaviors do to all children. We early childhood educators are in a good position to embrace the common cause of childhood and encourage others to do so as well.

Ethics and Justice for Every Child

It is because all children are affected in significant ways by negative social forces in the United States that I believe every early childhood

educator should be a vigilant advocate. We cannot deny that child circumstances vary widely, but we would do well to recognize that all children need teachers with a commitment to justice and ethics. All children
can better thrive in a classroom community in which positive human values and behaviors are modeled and reinforced. Hopefully, the children of
today, if they are fortunate enough to experience such classroom communities, will be the compassionate and civic-minded adults of tomorrow.

Linking Advocacy, Ethics, Justice, and Diversity

The conceptual framework on which this book is structured, as discussed in the introduction, is an imagined "tent" of child advocacy held
up by the conceptual "stakes" of commitment to social justice, adherence
to the ethics of teaching, and respect for diversity. Throughout this book
I will consider advocacy, ethics, justice, and respect for diversity to be
deeply interrelated—each depending on the understanding of and the
adherence to the others.

ADVOCACY: A TENT OF PROTECTION FOR CHILDREN

Advocacy for children has held an important place in early childhood
education for many years (Goffin & Lombardi, 1988; Robinson & Stark,
2005). The central concept of advocacy rests on the idea that childhood
educators, who encounter the barriers that can stand between children
and optimal development, should speak out and contribute to solutions
to political and social problems. In my first book, *Child Advocacy for Early
Childhood Educators* (1989), I defined child advocacy in this way:

> Child advocacy [is] a personal commitment to active involvement in the
> lives of children beyond remunerated professional responsibilities with the
> goal of enhancing the opportunities of those children for optimal personal
> growth and development. For early childhood professionals, advocacy is the
> way they take their dedication to the service of young children a step (or
> many steps) further to the point of becoming activists for young children.
> (p. 4)

Today, while my fundamental concept of child advocacy continues to
resonate with the above definition, I would make one significant change.
I think my original definition was affected by what was then current
thought that advocacy took place in settings *beyond the borders of schools
and classrooms.* I continue to believe that child advocacy in political (leg-
islative) and private-sector (business) settings is essential, closely related

to the act of teaching, and central to the improvement of child welfare in America (Goffin & Lombardi, 1988; Robinson & Stark, 2005). However, when I used the words "beyond remunerated responsibilities" I was overlooking the fundamental relationship of child advocacy to the practice of early childhood educators—the ways in which they approach their daily professional work with children. Today I would add this to my definition: Advocacy also can be integrated into classroom teaching and school-related interactions when teachers act upon their commitment to ethics, social justice, and respect for diversity in their daily practice.

Is Advocacy Too Controversial for Teachers?

Many teachers have asked me this question. They agree with the need for outspoken advocacy but do not feel that it is possible in their sites of practice. Some express discomfort with the idea of challenging district policies or raising controversial issues within the school. They say they are expected to be neutral in school or program politics; some express knowledge or fear of administrative retaliation when teachers involve themselves in contested areas that arise in the program, school, or district.

I think it is very important to be aware and respectful of the real risks that some teachers might take when they become stronger advocates in their schools. However, in this book, I hope to raise avenues for teacher advocacy that are *possible*, although never easy. Every early childhood educator has the power to decide where and when to stand up and be an advocate for children.

Advocacy: Traditional, Critical, and Participatory

This chapter is focused on *teacher intentions* that shape professional careers. The intention to be an advocate is never linear; we can never be sure of exactly what events will arise or of what the best ways will be to address problems that concern us. I pose three different kinds of advocacy that are interrelated—in many cases, teachers can select some parts of each to support an advocacy initiative in their schools.

Traditional child advocacy. Child advocacy has long been conceptualized as a way to call attention to the unmet needs of children and to work with others to make necessary social changes on their behalf (Fennimore, 1989; Robinson & Stark, 2005). For example, advocates might write letters to legislators, sign petitions circulated by professional groups and associations, or work with others to improve services for children.

Possibly, a group of advocates might volunteer to clean up an old dilapidated playground and petition the local government for funds for updated and safer equipment for child play.

Examples of traditional advocacy for teachers in schools might be to work with the Parent Association to set up a clothing donation collection room for children who are in need of warm winter attire, or to create avenues through which local businesses might donate needed supplies such as book bags, folders for home–school communications, paper, and crayons. Quite often, traditional advocacy can make a real difference for children without political controversy.

Critical child advocacy. Critical child advocacy often is focused on the forms of inequality that exist because an imbalance of power privileges some and marginalizes others (Ryan & Grieshaber, 2004). Critical advocacy is more likely to be controversial because it challenges an inequitable status quo. Those who feel criticized, or who feel that the inequities that benefit them or their children are justified, are likely to openly resist the changes suggested by critical advocates. This situation often arises in public conflicts over school resources that privilege some children over others in terms of status, funding, and resources (Fennimore, 2005).

An imbalance of power, resulting in privilege or oppression, often exists between the best interests of children and those of adults. Thus, educators who are critical child advocates frequently find themselves in conflict with opposing adults whose power is more influential than any possessed by the children and their families (Sensoy & DiAngelo, 2011). Consider, for example, a district in which a school board votes to eliminate play time from the kindergarten day so the children can spend more time on structured academic lessons. This initiative could possibly be backed by school administrators who stand to benefit from bonus pay if district test scores rise. A group of early childhood teachers in the district, uncomfortable with any mention of the above conflict of interest, decide to find a way to speak up for the children's developmental need for play. They are aware of the barriers they face as well as the risks in speaking out. What might they do?

Many teachers, in my experience, express hesitancy to be involved in critical advocacy for children in their site of practice because of perceived risks. However, when a situation is considered thoughtfully, there is almost always *something* that teachers can do so their voices will be heard. The teacher advocates in the above situation, for example, decide to ask for a meeting with their principal and early childhood curriculum supervisor. In that meeting they bring forth information on developmentally appropriate practices from the National Association for the Education of

Young Children (NAEYC) and pose several alternatives to the complete removal of play from the curriculum.

Ultimately, their early childhood supervisor is able to convince the school board and superintendent to reinstate play time in kindergarten 3 days a week. While this was not the complete solution sought by the teachers, they have helped the children as much as possible while retaining their professionalism and good relationship with their principal and curriculum supervisor.

Participatory advocacy in the workplace. All teachers have some opportunity to participate in meaningful ways in the democratic processes of their workplace. These may include scheduled faculty meetings, participation on committees, and formal or informal meetings with supervisors, administrators, and other teachers. Some districts and programs provide time during the school day for teachers to meet together to plan and discuss problems. Individual teachers can play a very important role in making sure that this is time well spent and focused on the children. Whatever the participatory opportunities might be, teachers who are participatory advocates take them seriously. They engage actively with others to express opinions, make contributions, and otherwise work for the betterment of the children.

While this kind of participation might seem obvious, in my experience many teachers are hesitant to speak up and express opinions during group meetings or activities. Discretion and common sense are always essential. However, the first step to participatory advocacy is to accept one's responsibility to fully engage with others to form a strong democratic community.

All advocacy is important. In conclusion, the intention to be an advocate during one's career opens up countless opportunities to be engaged and empowered. Teachers can find opportunities to be advocates every day; traditional, critical, and participatory advocacy are often interlinked as we respond to the demands of our daily lives as teachers. Under the "tent" of child advocacy, we can discover our best selves as teachers as we help all of our students to move forward in life.

SOCIAL JUSTICE: ESSENTIAL AND CONTROVERSIAL

This section will define social justice, examine recent controversy over the inclusion of social justice in teacher education, and relate social justice to ethics and respect for diversity in the classroom.

Defining Social Justice

Many theorists have sought to define social justice. John Rawls, in his theory of justice (1971, 2001), conceptualized social justice as the upholding of the common good by responsible citizens working in a spirit of fairness and cooperation within their social communities and professional institutions. His ideas continue to resonate with most conceptualizations of social justice as the existence of a society that is committed to fair and equal treatment of every individual. Such a society understands and values human rights and recognizes the dignity of every person (Zajda, Majhanovich, & Rust, 2006). Once a just society has established the resources to which each citizen should have equal access, it necessarily must be concerned when some citizens are able to gain little or no access to the needed resources (Rawls, 1971).

Social justice is defined not only as an idea but as an active *habit* that is "social" in two senses: It requires the skills necessary to inspire and work with others in a civil society, and it has a focus on the good of the community. As Novak (2000) indicates: "We must rule out any use of 'social justice' that does not attach itself to the habits (that is, virtues) of individuals. Social justice is a virtue, an attribute of individuals, or it is a fraud" (p. 11). Those who seek integrity must accept the responsibility for challenging the contradictions between social justice rhetoric and the realities of divisiveness and injustice within a society (Thrupp & Tomlinson, 2005). Further, they need to question the claims of others that they treat all people equally and fairly when they are in fact clearly acting otherwise (Bender-Slack & Raupach, 2008).

Why the Social Justice Controversy?

In the past few years, the centrality of social justice commitment to teaching has been challenged. Specifically, questions have been raised about the appropriateness of an emphasis on social justice in teacher education. The focus of much of this debate was on the documents of the National Council for the Accreditation of Teacher Education (NCATE) because of a reference to social justice as a possible consideration when evaluating a prospective candidate's disposition for teaching (Wilson, 2005). The controversy was based in large part on the idea that social justice is embedded in partisan politics—that it is "liberal" or "Democrat" rather than "conservative" or "Republican." Some feared that students in teacher education would be forced to adopt liberal political beliefs; they thus would be experiencing a form of political coercion that violated their first amendment rights and academic freedom (Wasley, 2006).

In response to the challenge, the leadership of NCATE first denied categorically that the organization had a mandatory standard for social justice (Applebaum, 2009). Then, as the controversy continued, the NCATE board voted to completely eliminate social justice language from its documents. It is left up to individual universities to decide whether social justice will be a focus of the teacher education program (Wilson, 2006).

THE RELEVANCE AND IMPORTANCE OF SOCIAL JUSTICE COMMITMENTS

I have been very concerned, since the above sequence of events, about the number of early childhood teachers and teacher educators I have encountered who believe that social justice is no longer an acceptable component of credentialed early childhood programs. I have been equally concerned about early childhood educators who seem to believe that the term *social justice* should be avoided because it generates too much controversy.

I believe there are two important steps that must be taken to reestablish the central relevance of social justice in teaching and teacher education. The first is to challenge the point of view that social justice in the United States is a political choice. I believe that commitment to social justice in this nation is a *political responsibility* for all citizens. While citizens retain the right to partisan loyalties, they also share the responsibility to uphold constitutional principles and related legal obligations. Where human rights and laws are violated, social justice concerns are essential regardless of personal and political affiliations. Teachers do not leave their American citizenship at the door of the school. They carry public trust for the well-being of vulnerable children and must be particularly mindful of laws, rights, and accompanying protections (Swadener, 2003).

The second step is to make it clear that academic freedom and the first amendment rights of students are a priority in teacher education. Students preparing for careers in education are encouraged to engage in critical thinking, to develop individual perspectives on social problems, and to articulate their positions freely in class discussions. The responsibility of teacher educators and professional developers, while avoiding coercion or abridgment of free speech, is to focus on the ways in which the ethics of our profession ultimately must guide all teachers to commitment to fairness, justice, and compassion for others.

PROFESSIONAL ETHICS: ESSENTIAL TO TEACHING PRACTICE

The discipline of ethics supports the intentions of educators who seek to do what is right and to recognize and alleviate what may be wrong in classrooms and schools. Ethics help us to judge and evaluate actions from a perspective of professional values and moral principles (Hopkins, 1997). Bakhtin, as discussed in Pollard (2011), emphasizes that every moment involves a choice of response for which we are responsible. As unique human beings, it is never right for us to abdicate our responsibility to do participatory thinking and to act on what we believe is right.

Ethics is the field of philosophy that asks questions about how morality should be *applied*. To be ethical is to be attentive to our guiding principles and to justify our actions in light of what we believe to be right (Taggart, 2011). We early childhood educators are so fortunate to have a well-developed and widely accepted professional code of ethics. This code, established by the National Association for the Education of Young Children (NAEYC, 2011), provides guidance on a wide variety of questions related to early childhood classroom practice. Its overarching goal is to uphold the human dignity of every child with whom we come into contact as educators; in every interaction, we must avoid doing harm and seek to do good (Feeney & Freeman, 2005).

Ethical codes are critical guides to right action on the part of those who are entrusted with the care of others (Hopkins, 1997). To be effective, however, they must be enacted by individuals and groups who understand them and see them as dynamic essentials to daily practice. The implementation of *intentional* ethics requires early childhood teachers to be very familiar with their written code and to consult it regularly when questions arise.

INTENTIONAL RESPECT FOR DIVERSITY IN EARLY CHILDHOOD CLASSROOMS

In this book, I am using the words *respect for diversity* to mirror those in the NAEYC Code of Ethical Conduct and Statement of Commitment (2011) (also referred to in this book as the Code of Ethics). In the past, the idea of "respecting" diversity may have been used by some to encourage admiration for human differences as something that should be enjoyed and celebrated (Castagno, 2009). At times, such broad (though valuable) goals have sidestepped controversy, thus silencing the problems of prejudice, discrimination, and institutional racism. This, in some cases, led to trivial approaches to multicultural education that neither acknowledged nor interrupted the pervasive forms of oppression that some children clearly were experiencing in their schools.

Still Fighting for Children's Rights

Multicultural education has had a pervasive and powerful impact on education in the United States. Yet, today, I see some truth in the statement that in many educational contexts the focus on multicultural education can be more a matter of rhetoric than reality (Boutte, 2008). It appears at times that the idea of multicultural education "has become both a popular catchphrase and an obsolete descriptor within educational settings" (Castagno, 2009, p. 43). Added to this problem is the fact that some educators are dismissing multicultural and anti-bias education as no longer necessary (De Gaetano, 2011).

I believe that the struggle to make schools places where all children are welcomed and respected, like the struggle for equal educational opportunity, is far from over. In fact, as Castagno (2009) has written, "given that the expected outcomes of multicultural education . . . have seen little improvement over the past few decades, we have to wonder whether multicultural education is actually occurring in schools" (p. 3). My intention is not to denigrate what has been accomplished by many great scholars, teachers, and leaders in multicultural education. Rather, I want to acknowledge the powerful challenges that continue to exist for everyone who is fighting for equality for all children in school and society.

Resistance and Progress

The evolution of multicultural education has greatly furthered the principle that all children must be protected from the harm of bias and discrimination, honored for the culture in which they live, and provided with the opportunity to be prepared in schools for meaningful lives as individuals and as culturally competent citizens. However, over more than half a century since the *Brown* decision, that principle still exists in contested grounds.

It continues to be up to us as teachers not only to acknowledge the differences that exist in every classroom but to address the ways in which those differences attract privilege or oppression. Our respect for diversity must be our fundamental respect for humanity and our refusal to participate in practices that harm the children in our care. We need to stand up to the resistance in school and society that continues to marginalize some children and to block their access to the fundamental opportunities that lead to positive life trajectories. Finally, our respect for diversity needs to be our ongoing willingness to acknowledge our own bias and to refuse to allow it to interfere with movement toward a society that considers equal treatment to be the irreducible right of every child.

The concepts of advocacy, justice, ethics, and respect for diversity are complex. The most important first step is to get excited about the ways in which standing up for something every day can illuminate and energize your daily life with children. Your enthusiasm, your vision, and your willingness to embrace powerful commitments will fill your classroom with hope and promise for all your students.

MEET OUR FOUR HYPOTHETICAL TEACHER-GUIDES

There are four hypothetical early childhood teacher-guides joining us throughout this book. These teacher-guides are a composite of the wonderful early childhood teachers with whom I have worked in many capacities and a wide variety of geographical and program or school settings over the years. The guides will provide examples of the thoughtful and complex ways in which they apply, in their early childhood sites of practice, the ideas in each of the following chapters. The reader will note that I have not identified a specific ethnic or racial identity for the guides. The reason for this is that I want to invite all readers to see themselves in each of the guides and to decide how they might act or think in a similar or different way based on their own experience and identity. I also hope that all readers, regardless of where they teach, will consider how the efforts of the teacher-guides might be enacted in their own particular classrooms and schools (including those serving wealthy or privileged children). The guides are constructed to demonstrate the deep complexities that are involved in the decisions and actions of any teacher who is determined to be ethical, just, and an advocate for all children.

Aanetra

Aanetra is certified in special and early childhood education, and has been teaching for the past 2 years in an inclusive state-funded suburban pre-K program. She is determined to focus on a number of tensions in parents, children, and other teachers that have arisen around the inclusion of children with special needs and children from a wide variety of economic backgrounds in her classroom as she works to promote respect for diversity and equality.

Emilio

Emilio is a bilingual 3rd-grade teacher in a high-poverty urban community. He feels pressured by his school district to improve the standardized test scores of his students at the expense of other subjects and culturally relevant activities. As a member of a family with mixed-immigration status in the United States, he feels committed to respecting his students with an authentic and relevant learning environment as he supports their academic success. He also wants to interrupt any resentment of their presence or of the support of their primary language in the school. Emilio thinks, *"Yo quiero mucho a mis estudiantes y quiero que sean exitosos en la escuela. Entiendo y respeto sus culturas y quiero que otros en la escuela también los respeten."* ["I love my students and I want them to be successful. I also want them to grow up respecting their culture, and I want others to respect it as well."]

Kira

Kira is certified in early childhood and elementary education, and is a new teacher in a "transitional" kindergarten–1st-grade classroom in a moderately sized city. (Her students were in kindergarten last year and deemed "not ready" for 1st grade this year.) A philosophy major who graduated with certification and a master's degree in education from an alternative teacher preparation program, she is determined to ethically address what she feels is the deficit approach to the ways her students are conceptualized, talked about, and treated in her school.

Jordan

Jordan has been the head teacher for the mixed-age, 3- to 5-year-old room in his small rural child-care center for the past 5 years. His differentiated curriculum is designed to provide early kindergarten experiences for the older children, who subsequently spend a full year of kindergarten at the consolidated school district an hour away by school bus. The district has found it best to delay the long day and school entry until the children are closer to 6 years of age. Jordan has become skilled at making his curriculum accessible to children at a variety of ages. Jordan is a natural leader who speaks openly with his colleagues and director about his beliefs and commitments to ethics and social justice.

All four teachers will provide us with opportunities for thought and reflection as we consider the actions they take in their classrooms and schools to stand up for their students.

SOME PRACTICAL IDEAS FOR GETTING STARTED

Some of you may already have begun to put your commitments and intentions in the areas of diversity, ethics, and justice to work in your professional settings. Others may very much want to do this, but feel unsure of where to start. Here are some suggestions.

Begin systematic observation in your classroom and school. What emerges in the interactions and conversations of your students? Are they kind to one another? What sorts of exclusions or conflicts do you see as they play or work together? What beliefs about diversity and differences emerge in group discussions? Take brief daily notes to get a stronger picture of the relationships and attitudes of the children.

Open conversation with colleagues. What emerges in the interactions and conversations of your colleagues? Do you hear voices of advocacy? Are you aware of labeling or negative assumptions that relate to critical advocacy? As you observe and think about this, start to get ideas about how you might talk more about your commitments to social justice, ethics, and respect for diversity in your classroom. You may want to let all of your colleagues know that you have placed the NAEYC Code of Ethics in an accessible place in your classroom for reference. Possibly you could suggest a 10-minute weekly discussion of an ethical issue before or after your work with the children.

Start a journal. This is a good time to keep a journal in which you jot down incidents, expressions, or other events in your classroom that relate to diversity, ethics, and social justice. Share your experiences and interests with like-minded colleagues—and use your journal to inform your daily practice.

Strengthen your voice. Think about meetings, committees, and informal discussions as an opportunity to build your identity as a teacher committed to advocacy, ethics, social justice, and respect for diversity. Start to explore ways of sharing your opinions and ideas with others.

Questions for Discussion

1. Think ahead to the day that you retire from your career in the service of young children. What do you most want people to remember about your intentions as an educator?

2. How frequently do you have time to think about justice and ethics in your daily practice? How might you make these concepts more "present" every day?
3. How have you been thinking about the concept of diversity up to this point in your career? What do you think of the idea of diversity as the norm?
4. Are there any ethical issues in your educational past or present that you strongly feel should be addressed by your profession?
5. Is "social justice" a term with which you are politically comfortable as an educator? Why or why not?

Two

Teacher Talk Is Teacher Action!

All teachers have a powerful and readily available tool to support their daily intentions to enact ethics and justice in their classrooms. That tool is their "teacher talk"—the language that they use in daily life to discuss and describe the children they teach. Your words are with you every day—in and out of the classroom. This chapter will focus on the ways in which you characterize and talk about your children in your professional setting.

How does the way you talk about your students outside the classroom affect the way you teach? All of your words count. They embody and enact the ways in which you choose to see your students, and the ways in which you want others to see them. All of the good intentions you have to be an ethical advocate who respects diversity must be reflected in the words you use to describe your students. This chapter will connect teacher talk and teacher action. As we explore the importance of educational language, our hypothetical teacher-guides will be with us to demonstrate the efforts they make to counteract deficit-based talk about children in their schools.

THE IMPORTANCE OF TEACHER TALK

As a teacher educator, I have spent a great deal of time supervising student teachers in urban, rural, and suburban schools. Over the years, as I listened to the talk of educators in schools, I became increasingly aware of the routine use of deficit terminology and denigrating descriptions of children in many school settings:

"Low-income students"
"Parents who don't care"
"Homes that don't value education"
"Kids who start school way behind"
"The kids who are poor have limited vocabularies"
"This school is filled with at-risk kids"

I realized that many sincere and dedicated educators did not see an ethical conflict in the use of deficit-based descriptions of children and families. The use of such language in schools—especially schools serving a large number of immigrants, children of color, or children who were poor—appeared to be an accepted norm. As my interest in this topic grew, I started to raise it for discussion with the teachers in my graduate classes. Many readily admitted that such talk was commonplace in their schools, particularly in the teachers' lounge. However, they believed that what they said outside of the classroom did not influence the way they or others treated children in the classroom.

Does what we say outside our classroom have an impact on what happens to our students? I became fascinated with that question and undertook a study of linguistic theory to find the answer. The more I read, the greater my realization that every word we say about our students has a very important impact on their well-being.

In his influential book *How to Do Things with Words*, linguistic philosopher John Austin (1962) indicated that words were not so much descriptive as active—they were always *doing something*. When asked, "Can saying it make it so?" Austin replied with his belief that "the uttering of words is . . . *the* leading incident in the performance of an act" (p. 8, emphasis in original). Similarly, John Searle, in *Speech Acts: An Essay in the Philosophy of Language* (1969), called words a form of action and described them as *speech acts* that not only made things happen, but made it likely that they would continue to happen in exactly the same way (Fennimore, 2008).

Once we realize that the language that we use to describe children is a behavior with significant repercussions, we must recognize the relationship of our teacher talk to the ethical standards that exist for all our professional behaviors. The words we choose can enhance the lives of children in our care or bring them harm. For example, let's think about a hypothetical teacher who calls his students "slow" or "delayed" or "unmotivated" in the teachers' lounge. His words are acting to create the likelihood that those listening also will begin to think of the students in that light. In some present or future situation, the listeners might act with lowered expectations or some other form of negativity toward the children under discussion. The children would be affected by the negativity and lowered expectations, and might respond with deep discouragement about themselves as learners. Once said, words have an impact far beyond our reach.

As we consider the above situation, we also need to think about the way we *ourselves* are influenced by the way we talk about our students. The ingrained habit of thoughtful reflectiveness on anything we say about our students strengthens our professional practice. When we regularly speak respectfully about students' strengths we are much more likely to see and act on them in our classrooms. Likewise, routine negative denigration of our students outside the classroom will have an inevitable effect on the way we interact with them in the classroom. Our words create an important aura around everything we do and say as teachers.

LANGUAGE IS A SOCIAL ACT

Vygotsky emphasized language as a socially generated phenomenon; it is our tool for communication with others and *always has the intended outcome of influencing others* (Berk & Winsler, 1995). Bakhtin (1986) explains how all of our words emerge from that totality of a dynamic interpersonal exchange. The words that we use when we speak have been taken from others and also will be used by others. Once used, our words no longer belong just to us.

The term *discourse* refers to the consideration of language as a social practice. As we talk with others, we represent our personal perception of social realities and we also take a personal position on social problems (Thomas, 2011). Through these representations we publicly construct an identity for ourselves as well as for others. Thus, our discourse about our students is never "neutral"; we are saying who we are as teachers as we also seek to influence the ways in which we and our students are perceived by our listeners (Goffman, 1959). Ultimately, our discourse constructs the language environment of our schools and programs.

Let's use the example of educational discourse about disability. The field of early childhood education has been steeped in a deficit model of understandings about disability, which often is reduced to a set of deficiencies and problems inherent in the bodies of individuals (Ferri & Bacon, 2011). This deficit model is not inevitable; it represents a choice of language and a thus a social choice of position toward the existence of disability.

It is entirely possible to construct a different disability discourse—one that considers people with disabilities as competent; their differences are interesting and have the capacity to enrich the lives of others (Ferri & Bacon, 2011). Such an approach would focus in some ways on the differences in bodies and minds of students with disabilities, but would focus more on the similarities and strengths that connect all who experience human life (Danforth & Gabel, 2006). This alternative form of discourse would eliminate the idea that "there is something wrong with a person with a disability." Considering the dynamic social nature of discourse, our positive approach to disability would construct our identity as teachers who respect human differences; it also would construct the identity of the person with the disability as *able,* albeit in different ways, to live a life that is valued and should be respected equally with all other life.

Aanetra Focuses on Parents and Makes a Plan

Aanetra has become increasingly aware of a number of stratifications in the suburban community in which she has been a teacher in a federally funded inclusive pre-K program. Although the pre-K program is open to all the children in the suburb, one of the federal funding requirements was that a percentage of the children meet lower income criteria and that another percentage have identified disabilities. Aanetra is concerned, as families and caregivers drop children off and wait to pick them up, that they tend to associate in small groups—those whose children fall into the lower income and disabilities categories tend to stay to themselves; those associated with the more affluent children also stand apart and speak only with one another.

Aanetra wants to create a community of parents and learners, and decides first to do something about parent talk she frequently overhears about "the special-needs kids." She gets the feeling that a number of the parents tolerate the presence of children with disabilities in the program, but do not see those children as equal to their own. Aanetra is planning the first of three workshops, all of which the program requires parents to attend. She decides to focus on disability-related identity and language.

As she plans the workshop, Aanetra makes sure that she assigns each parent to a small group that includes parents with higher and lower incomes as well as parents of children with disabilities. The workshop will be called "What's My Name?" Parents will first talk in small groups about the origins of their own first names. Then they will create hypothetical first names for themselves based on something they like to do and think they are good at doing. Following this, all the parents will circulate, introducing themselves to one another with their hypothetical names: "Hi, I'm Mountain Climber"; "Hi, I'm Pet Shelter Volunteer"; "Hi, I'm Good Cook"; "Hi, I'm Great Listener."

Aanetra will follow this activity, which is always fun for everyone, with a short talk on how good it is to have the power to name ourselves based on our strengths and competencies. She will ask the parents to think briefly about the ways in which they would not identify themselves—possibly faults or things that they cannot do very well. Then, the parents in small groups will give their own children hypothetical names based on their strengths and competencies, and share them with their small groups. Aanetra will end the workshop by listening to the new names created for all the children and indicate her determination as the teacher to avoid child labeling and to recognize child abilities. She will invite the parents to think in similar ways and avoid ableism by seeing all children as competent learners and speaking about them with that in mind.

UNDERSTANDING THE EDUCATIONAL LANGUAGE ENVIRONMENT

It is helpful to think of any language we use that is related to our students and our professional responsibilities as our *educational language*. This differs from our casual social language because it is part of the work to which we are dedicated and for which we are remunerated. In my book *Talk Matters: Refocusing the Language of Public Schooling* (2000), I define educational language as the way in which educators discuss, describe, categorize, and verbally expect behavior and achievements from the children in their classrooms. It is "what is said, how it is said, why it is said, and the intended and unintended outcomes of saying it" (p. 2).

The educational language that is used by everyone in the school creates the *language environment* (Postman & Weingartner, 1969). The language environment in any early childhood setting is unique; it is composed of what all the professionals in that setting are saying to one another every day. Visitors to schools quickly can perceive the language environment—it tends to paint a clear picture of the attitudes of teachers and administrators toward their students. Thus we never *just talk!* The totality of our educational language takes on a life of its own and has a tangible impact on everyone who hears us.

When we listen carefully to the discourse that is utilized in a school or program, we can begin to critically analyze the educational language environment. In *critical discourse analysis*, what is left out and not said can be as important as what is said (Johnson & Stephens, 2012). Why, for example, would an educator bring to our attention that a certain child has a parent in prison, but leave out the fact that the other parent is working exceptionally hard to help that child in every possible way? Or, why would an administrator indicate that his high-poverty school has inferior students, but leave out the fact that a good percentage of the students are performing on a very high level? In a different vein, why might an educator attribute the success of students in her affluent school to "parents who care about their children and value schooling," but leave out the fact that there has been a high incidence of bullying in that school? These are *choices* that reflect the ways in which the educators want their students to be viewed by others.

We need to ask why these educators are choosing to make either the positive or negative attributes more visible to others. The ways in which we discuss children may be a matter of habit to some degree, but ultimately we need to look beneath the surface for the political interplay of social privilege and oppression in our language environment and discourse about our students. It may be unsettling to realize that we are choosing to lower the perceptions of others about the students we teach, but that realization opens the door to reflection and a different set of choices.

Kira Stands Up to Negative Talk About Children in Public Housing

---

From her first day in her transitional kindergarten, Kira became aware of problems in the ways her students were viewed and discussed in the school. As a new teacher, she did not feel comfortable with the idea of confronting teachers who expressed negative thoughts and low expectations for her children. She acknowledged that the children had exhibited some learning and behavior problems last year, and that she found them challenging at times. But she also enjoyed them and respected their resiliency. They deserved a new chance to be free from old labels this year!

Much of the deficit terminology Kira has heard about her students seems to focus on their poverty; most of the children reside in nearby public housing. Kira decides that, in addition to her own ethical language about her students, she is going to try to change the way that other teachers perceive and talk about their lives and abilities. Last summer, Kira had made the decision to take a day to visit the children's neighborhood. There was a warm and friendly community representative in the housing complex, who introduced her to many people and showed her many resources that existed for the children and their families.

One of the most interesting things Kira learned was that a group of artists in the area had developed a free summer art program for the children in the community. Last summer, quite a few of her students had participated in the program, which had focused on art forms in their environment. The community representative showed her a beautiful model of the neighborhood, complete with the playground that had been built with the help of community activists. All of the children in the summer program had helped to make the model.

Kira was allowed to borrow the model, and she worked with the principal and school librarian to display it in the library for a few months. She took a picture of her whole class in front of the display and put it on her hallway bulletin board. Under the picture, she placed sentence strips with the comments the children made about the display. For the remainder of the year, whenever she heard a negative reference to her students or the housing project she would say something like, "Did you see their wonderful artistic replica of their neighborhood? I am so proud of them and they are proud of their work."

THE CULTURAL POLITICS OF LANGUAGE

Critical discourse analysis helps us to understand the cultural politics of language (Cohen, 2010). Sociocultural theory supports the idea that cultural politics play out in the ways that student identities (and the parts of student identities we choose to emphasize) are mediated in the context of schooling. The labeling of children is central to the idea of cultural politics—labels are dynamic actions, reactions, and interactions that often determine success or failure in schooling (Varenne & McDermott, 1998). When we use labels we are using our power over others—to determine, for example, whose exceptionality is positive ("gifted") and whose exceptionality reflects supposed inferiority ("socially and emotionally disturbed"). We are neither neutral nor passive when we ascribe characteristics to children—we are making cultural and political decisions about how they will be represented in school and society (Cohen, 2010).

Language Reflects Teacher Culture

Vygotsky, in his analysis of language as a social medium, believed that language is the product of the social history of a cultural group (Berk & Winsler, 1995). Teachers have all been raised and educated in specific cultural structures characterized by repeated thoughts and actions about and toward others (Warren & Webb, 2007). Their educational language inevitably will reflect their cultural experiences and beliefs.

Many teachers in America are in classrooms with children whose cultural experiences are different from their own. In these cases, the teachers inevitably will position and define themselves in relationship to the diversities they are called upon to understand (Cummins, 1989). Their educational language, as we discussed earlier, will reflect the identity they construct for themselves as well as the identities they construct for their students.

Critical discourse analysis in such situations is helpful. Are students routinely discussed as deficient, or unmotivated, or unintelligent? Any school language environment characterized by habitual deficit-based representations of students raises the question of teacher–student cultural misalignment. This misalignment may privilege some students (i.e., students whose lives are culturally similar to those of the teachers) and oppress others (such as the students whose lives and experiences create a position of bias on the part of the teacher).

Emilio Forms a Coalition and Makes a Plan

As a 3rd-grade bilingual teacher in a high-poverty urban school, Emilio is very uncomfortable with the language environment of his school. He thinks it reflects a general bias toward the children of the poor as well as a specific bias toward the children in the bilingual program. Emilio hears talk in the teachers' lounge expressing disagreement with bilingual education because "the kids should just be expected to speak English once they get to school." He was very upset one day to hear a child spoken of as a "wetback"; the speaker did not realize Emilio was in the room.

Emilio is good friends with several other teachers in the building. He invites them to lunch in his classroom and expresses his discomfort with the persistently negative talk about the children in the school. Emilio also talks about the disrespect toward the children in the bilingual program. He shares his idea: The assembled group could join together and agree to consistently model interest in Spanish and positive talk about the children in general.

The group comes to consensus around two ideas. The first is that, with Emilio as volunteer translator, they routinely will each place some Spanish words under the English words on their hallway bulletin boards. The second is that they will shape their responses to deficit-based comments about the children in the school in three ways: (1) They will indicate that they are committed to teaching the children well; (2) they will identify a positive ability or characteristic of the children; and (3) they will acknowledge the difficulties of teaching and encourage their colleague to be positive and hopeful. *"Yo quiero darle a estos estudiantes todas las oportunidades que pueda. Mis estudiantes están trabajando muy duro este año. No siempre es fácil ver algunos de los obstáculos que tienen nuestros estudiantes en sus vidas. Tenemos que creer que nuestros esfuerzos están haciendo una diferencia."* ["I want to give these students all the opportunities that I can. My class is working so hard this year. Of course it is not easy for us to see some of the struggles our students have in their lives. We have to believe that our efforts are making a real difference."]

DESIGN YOUR EDUCATIONAL LANGUAGE TO AVOID CATEGORIZING CHILDREN IN SCHOOLS

The educational language you use today has been shaped by many forces, including your own teacher preparation and the culture of the school or program in which you work or have had field experiences. All teachers undoubtedly have some forms of bias and also encounter bias in the attitudes and expressions of other professionals. I believe that every one of us can benefit a great deal from reflecting on our own talk about children in the context of our social and cultural experiences.

Categorizing Children in Schools

We humans have the tendency to "think with our categories" (Postman & Weingartner, 1969). Once we categorize children in schools, we tend to consistently think of them in one way rather than another. In my book *Talk Matters* (2000), I identified three ways in which children tend to be categorized in schools. These are: (1) deficit terminology (broad deficit-based generalizations about children with certain cultural or racial characteristics), (2) labels and scores on standardized test scores (achievement-based characteristics), and (3) confidential family information (access to family information that can raise or lower the status of children within schools and programs). Most teachers in my graduate classes find it interesting and helpful to analyze the language environment of their schools using these three categories as a guide.

Listen to the Talk!

Listen attentively to discussions about children in your school. If you are aware of deficit terminology ("at risk," "Title I kids," "free-lunch students," "lower kids"), take note of the terms you hear most frequently. Also, think about labels and any groupings based on assessments or standardized test scores ("proficient kids," "disabled," "bottom-level readers") and take note of them as well. Then, think about the ways in which confidential information about families can become a categorization ("single-parent families," "public assistance families," "parents who care/don't care," "parent in jail," "professional parent"). This will give you a good portrait of the language environment of your school or program. You then can start to think about how you might have a greater impact on that language environment.

Re-naming Our Categories

Johnston (2004) developed the idea of "noticing and naming" as a literacy strategy. Teachers were encouraged to pay close attention to the reading strategies that students were using and to name them for the students so they would be more aware of a competency that was helping them. Laman, Miller, and Lopez-Robertson (2012) extended the concept of noticing and naming to the importance of noticing and naming the skills of children that defy the labels to which they have been assigned in school. ("She is labeled socially and emotionally disturbed, but when she is really interested in an activity she cooperates so well with the other kids.") You can notice, name, and challenge the ways in which categories influence your thinking—and you can help others to expand their perception of children as well. It is always possible to identify new names based on what you see in your classroom every day.

Jordan Starts to Notice and Name

Jordan has been head teacher for the 3- to 5-year-old children in his rural child-care center for the past 5 years. Like many of the teachers in the center, he has become accustomed to thinking about the children in certain ways. The center has a sliding-fee scale and receives government funding for the children of migrant workers and those whose families are below the poverty line. Some of the children live on farms; others live in small homes or trailers that are quite remote. If the families do not own cars, the children rarely leave their home settings to go to libraries or stores or other places in town.

Since Jordan began working for his graduate degree at a local university, he has become fascinated by the ways in which the social justice teaching discussed in his courses applies to his child-care setting. He realizes that he and the other teachers routinely have been referring to the children's "lack of experience" and "limited environments." He has begun to realize that they have been devaluing their own rural lifestyles as well as those of the children—rural as compared with suburban and urban has taken on the habitual characterization of "less than."

Jordan asked the director if he might have 15 minutes to speak at the next faculty meeting. In his center, teachers are always welcome to ask for time to share ideas or raise issues for consideration. Jordan talks about the beauty of the rural area, the importance of farming, and the contribution of the migrant workers. He suggests that everyone start to notice what is interesting and beneficial about rural life in a small community. "Let's stop calling rural life 'limited' and let's start noticing and naming all the things that our children know and can do because of their rural cultures and lifestyles." He places several large Post-it charts in the faculty room with some pens and suggests that for the next month faculty notice, name, and write down the competencies, abilities, and interests of all the students. For example, many of them help farm and care for animals; others have learned a lot about streams, plants, and wooded areas. Jordan hopes that this will be a good beginning to enriching and changing the language environment of his center.

FREQUENTLY ASKED QUESTIONS

My research and writing in the area of educational language have given me the opportunity to talk with many teachers in professional development or at conferences about this issue. I have found over the years that there are two questions that almost any group of teachers will raise. They are good questions!

Can't We Tell the Truth?

Many teachers have asked whether I am suggesting that it is unethical to be truthful about the problems presented by students. Do I expect them to pretend that the children do not have serious problems? That they are all academically on target? My response is that it is appropriate and necessary to discuss specific problems in the context of seeking a solution. What must be avoided are broad, biased generalizations about certain groups of children.

For example, saying, "I just can't find a way to motivate my children in math right now, so I am searching for new techniques" is different from saying, "My students are not motivated to learn math." Likewise, saying, "I am struggling to find a way to help my children to develop stronger self-control" is very different from saying, "This is the toughest group of kids I have ever encountered." Central to the discussion of child-related problems should be the strong and concerned voices of teachers who hold themselves responsible for addressing the needs of children, however problematic, in a positive way.

What About Venting?

We educators have difficult jobs and we do encounter problems. At times, despite our very best efforts, we become frustrated and discouraged. Can't we share our feelings with colleagues to gain some support? My answer is, yes, we all need to share our experiences, and we all need to vent! Let's say, for example, that you have been making many efforts to give extra support to a child in class. However, you discover one day that the child's parent has indicated to the program director that you are "not doing enough." You might be furious! You have 30 children in the group, you work for hours before and after school to create a wonderful curriculum, and you indeed have done a great deal to help this child! What might you do?

My advice is that we should seek reciprocal relationships with a few trusted colleagues who share our dedication and commitment to ethical talk. We can agree that, at appropriate times and behind closed doors, we will listen to and support one another when we are upset or angry or frustrated. However, we will do this with the mutual understanding that we are venting with one another in confidence because our emotions or concerns in a certain situation require us to seek support and counsel. We are talking about our challenges and the way they are making us feel, which is very different from deficit-based or denigrating talk about our students and their families.

TALK IS ADVOCACY IN ACTION

Language is a fascinating area from a theoretical and philosophical perspective. It is also a critically important component of every school and program serving children. Language can convey our professionalism, our sense of efficacy, and our hopes and dreams for our students. It also can, however, convey bias, low expectations, and harmful labels. It is up to each and every one of us to consciously shape our professional use of language to reflect our deepest beliefs about social justice for all children.

As you can see from the actions of our teacher-guides, commitment to positive talk about children, interventions in our classrooms, and active advocacy are intertwined. The teachers knew it would take more than speaking positively themselves; they had to find concrete ways to lead others by example. It takes critical advocacy to see the power and positioning in language; it takes traditional advocacy to think of something helpful that can be done. We engage in participatory advocacy by modeling positive and productive language about children, and by taking advantage of situations in which our voice can be heard and make a difference.

SOME PRACTICAL IDEAS FOR GETTING STARTED

Many teachers and graduate students have told me that the concept of changing talk in their schools seems very complex. They have so many daily responsibilities in their classrooms that they just do not feel they have the time to address such a big issue. I suggest starting with small steps and waiting for opportunities to enlarge the impact they can have in the area of language about children in school. Following are some ways to get started.

Increase Your Own Language Awareness

This is a good time to start listening more closely to what is said and what is not said in your school or program. Be a language observer: How are the children represented in the ways that professionals talk with one another. What seems positive? What might you want to change if you could? Also, of course, this is a good time to be more aware of the ways in which you talk about children yourself. Has any bias crept into your descriptions of children? Have you been affected over time by the social, cultural, and political dimensions of the language environment of your school? Just start by taking some time to listen a bit more carefully to yourself and to others.

Develop a Personal Strategy for Responding to Bias

If you become aware that you are drawn into negative conversations about children, this is a good time to think about a personal strategy for responding to bias. For example, let's say that two other teachers on your grade level seem to be complaining constantly about the quality of students currently attending the school. You can think of a response to this that is neither argumentative nor confrontational. If you are at a grade-level meeting to discuss curriculum, and a negative conversation about the quality of the students arises, you might say, "These are some interesting problems. I want to help solve them—what might we do today to get started?" At some point you may want to take a stronger stance of advocacy, but many teachers like to start with making a positive comment with the intent of moving from deficit-based talk to helpful solutions.

Follow the Teacher-Guides

In this chapter, our teacher-guides gave us some good ideas for language-related strategies. If you are teaching a group of children that is considered "low" or "less than," try demonstrating projects or assignments that honor their home environments and growth as learners. Bring these to the attention of others in the school and model your own positive and respectful talk about the students. If you are concerned about the language environment in general, you might see whether you can form a small coalition of like-minded colleagues and decide on a positive and structured approach to negative comments about the students. At some point you might have the chance to do a workshop for teachers or parents that addresses the issue of language. Finally, taking your own steps to notice child competencies and give new names to children with deficit-based labels will give you a great start in the right direction.

Questions for Discussion

1. How would you characterize the language environment of your school or program? If a visitor came to listen to what educators were saying about the children during the day, what impression would the visitor come away with?
2. How much do you think the classification of children does or does not affect the ways in which they are spoken about by educators?
3. What do you think about the idea that denigrating or deficit-based talk about children outside the classroom does not affect the ways in which children are treated inside the classroom? Do you agree or disagree? Why?
4. What goals would you set for yourself in terms of the ways in which you describe children? In terms of the ways you tend to respond to deficit-based conversations of others?
5. The teacher-guides in this chapter went well beyond their classroom responsibilities to be language-related advocates for their students. Would you consider such actions a possibility for you in your own school? Why or why not?

THREE

Intentional Respect for Diversity

Every early childhood teacher encounters much diversity that must be acknowledged and included in daily practice. This chapter will approach diversity, multicultural education, anti-bias education, and culturally responsive teaching through the lens of dynamic and applicable concepts and principles for teachers and classrooms today. Respect for diversity will be considered central to integrating all these approaches into effective daily teaching practices in classrooms.

DIVERSITY IS ON THE INCREASE IN THE UNITED STATES

America has always been characterized by diversity, but today the forms of diversity are expanding. Our public schools are now more racially, culturally, and linguistically diverse than ever before. While increasing diversity may be more evident in urban areas, our schools in suburban and rural areas also are increasingly diverse (Nieto, 2012). In addition, almost 4 million legal immigrants settled in the United States between 2000 and 2004; about 1,000 legal immigrants and a large but undetermined number of illegal immigrants enter the United States every year (Banks, 2007b).

According to the Census Bureau (2010) the Asian population grew faster than any other major race group in the United States during 2000–2010. In that same time period the Hispanic population grew by 43%. The non-Hispanic, White population, while still numerically and proportionally the largest major race and ethnic group, is growing at the slowest pace. This trend could mean that the number of students of color might equal or exceed the number of White students within 1 or 2 decades (Banks, 2007a). These figures mean that all teachers must be prepared for diverse learners, and all children must be prepared to live in an increasingly diverse nation.

As Banks (2007a) indicated:

> The rich cultural, ethnic, social-class and linguistic diversity of students in U.S. schools presents serious challenges to teachers and other educators. It

also provides rich opportunities to create a nation-state in which diversity is valued and greatly enriches American society. (p. xi)

Whoever you are and wherever you teach, respect for diversity is central to your effectiveness and ultimate success.

Culture, Ethnicity, and Race

School is a place where cultures intersect; teaching and learning must take place through the lens of relationships that reflect cultural understandings. *Culture* might be regarded as lifestyle, learned traditions, and habitual ways of thinking, feeling, and behaving. Culture is intricately linked to *ethnicity*—perceived membership in a social group that has distinct characteristics such as family structure, physical appearance, first language, and faith tradition. *Race*, although it is often a core focus of cultural and ethnic discourse, is in fact a construct of society that describes people by their outward appearance only (Richards, 2011). Culture, ethnicity, and race intertwine to create a lived experience for students and teachers in the classroom.

Including Whiteness in Diversity

As we approach the demographics and challenges ahead, I propose that we purposefully include all groups, including Whites, as part of the *norm of diversity* in the United States. Specifically, this would eliminate the idea of people who are White as the "norm" and other groups as "diverse." As a White teacher educator, I very frequently encounter students, teachers, and administrators who continue to think that diversity has only one meaning—"not White." They might indicate, for example, that their own schools "do not have diversity" because there are no students of color. Conversely, if they are in a segregated school enrolling only children of color, they might say, "I am working with a diverse population." There are many variations on what is said, but the bottom line is the assumption that White is the norm and non-White is diverse.

At this point in time, I consider the "not-White" conceptualization of diversity to be quite problematic. It retains a generalized assumption of Whiteness as the nonproblematized norm of the nation, while ignoring many variations (such as poverty) that exist within the White population. Continued centralization of White as the norm sidesteps the significance of changing demographics and fosters racism by marginalizing all people with darker skin as the "different other." Educators who hold on to the idea that diversity is related only to skin color are not acknowledging many other diversities, including language, disability, religion, sexual orientation, gender, ethnicity, age, and socioeconomic status. These differences also encounter significant bias and require recognition. The solution, I would suggest, starts with the inclusion of everyone in the United States in the norm of diversity.

What I do. In consideration of the above dilemma, I have changed my approach to diversity in my university courses and professional development. I indicate right away that I will not consider Whiteness as the norm—thus there will be no need to think about "who is and who is not diverse." My perspective will be that we are all diverse and part of the diversity of this nation. I explain that our work together will be complex because we will be thinking critically about unique diversity histories with an eye toward privilege, power, cultural domination, and oppression. There will be a lot of space for critical analysis and different perspectives, but our goal is focused and determined progress toward equal treatment and equal opportunity for every group.

Honoring Identity and Recognizing Oppression

I want to make it clear that my suggestion of a common bond of diversity is completely unrelated to "colorblindness" (the questionable claim that we do not notice and respond to skin color or other differences). It is critically important, as I see it, that differences are noticed, acknowledged, and talked about. In addition to claims of "not seeing differences," we need to be concerned about "dysconsciousness," or the artificial celebration of differences that obscures acknowledgment of inequity and discrimination (King, 1991). We as educators have the responsibility to acknowledge and stand up to racism, colonization, historical oppression, and hate in the United States.

Further, I believe it remains very important for different cultural and ethnic groups to articulate their unique identities and to speak out against forces that marginalize or discriminate against them. We can seek greater unity as people without losing the important identities that are central to our human experience. Some groups must indeed continue to fight for their very survival, and we all have a responsibility to work together for the common good.

WHAT IS MULTICULTURAL EDUCATION?

Multicultural education has its roots in the racial inequities that fueled the civil rights movement of the 1960s and has gone through many transformations since its inception. It continues to seek to "reform the school and other educational institutions so that students from diverse, ethnic, and social class groups will experience educational equality" (Banks & Banks, 1995, p. 3). Within that defined goal, there are innumerable ways for educators to respond to the demands of the diversity and multiplicity of interests in their own settings.

Since its inception in the 1960s, multicultural education has made a tremendous contribution to our acceptance and understanding of multiple differences in the classroom (Koppelman, 2011). The focus of multicultural education has expanded over the years to include many groups and interests, thus increasing our awareness of inclusiveness as a critical component of excellent education (Castagno, 2009). Multicultural education is in many ways a reform movement, challenging the assumption that all the diverse groups in the United States must either assimilate into one single culture or be viewed as inferior. Our nation is characterized by diverse people unified in common purpose; multicultural education has reinforced the idea that pluralism of identity and perspective is of great importance to our nation. It also has reinforced a greater national acknowledgment of discrimination and a renewal of commitment to equal opportunity as essential to the education of all citizens (Banks, 2007a; Koppelman, 2011).

MULTICULTURAL EDUCATION STARTS WITH INTENTIONS

As a multicultural teacher educator and professional developer, I often encounter frustration in my students or the teachers with whom I work. They feel that many books and articles about multicultural education are obscure and do not outline exactly what actually should be done. The complexities of teaching about and responding to multiple forms of diversity can seem overwhelming. I think this is why many of the educators with whom I work say, "Please, just tell us what to do in our classrooms."

Unfortunately, I believe that it is impossible for me to meet that request. The topic of diversity is highly complex and cannot be reduced to prescriptive methods and isolated lessons and activities for children. When teachers want to commit to multicultural education, they first must reflect on and establish their *intentions*. What will they consider as their most important areas of daily focus, and how will they intend to integrate those areas of focus into their curriculum and interactions with their students? Once their commitments are established, they naturally will grow increasingly aware of opportunities for multicultural teaching and learning.

Many excellent early childhood resources are available to teachers— technology easily places a lot of them at our fingertips. There is also a wealth of wonderful books for children that explore many different aspects of diversity. Teachers with the intention of infusing multicultural learning in their classrooms must start by knowing their students well and acknowledging students' differences as well as strengths. With that information in mind, they not only will select appropriate activities and resources, but also will evaluate and modify them so that they are relevant and meaningful for the children in the classroom.

The blend of intentions and good use of multicultural resources will help teachers develop many strategies for approaching diversity in their classrooms. Such strategies will support the expansion of cultural competence in their students—they will better come to know themselves and others in meaningful ways. The materials and activities that teachers select can go well beneath the surface to also help the children become interested in the idea of *activism*—working with others to solve problems and create a culture of fairness. There are many ways, even when teaching young children, to create understanding of the historical oppression of some groups of people. This can motivate their sense of justice and enhance development of their interest in making the world a better place (Perry & Fraser, 1993).

Aanetra's Literacy Focus on Competence Within Differences

Aanetra is continuing to resolve challenges and conflicts related to the inclusion of children with special needs and economic disparities in her suburban pre-K program. Her parent workshop on labeling was well received, although she continues to overhear some negative comments in conversations about children. She also is noticing that some of her students are experiencing subtle exclusions from other children. Aanetra has used discretionary federal program funds to order a variety of children's books related to diversity. She talks things over with her reading coach and identifies ways that she can use the books to meet the literacy goals of the preschool program as well as multicultural education. Aanetra does not want to limit her focus to disabilities or socioeconomic status; rather, she wants to present her students with many ways of thinking about diversity.

Aanetra Conceptualizes Her Approach. Aanetra first thinks about some of the diversities that are present in her classroom. One of her students recently moved to the United States from Pakistan, and his English skills are in development. One of her students has two mothers who recently were married. She has heard some Disney-influenced talk among the girls about being "princesses" and also has heard a few boys say, "only boys can play here." There is a significant economic gap between the most and least affluent families in her program, and two of her students are adopted. Aanetra thinks these diversities will provide a rich opportunity for her new focus.

Aanetra Makes a Plan. Aanetra takes time to reflect carefully on the focus over the coming weeks. She looks at her collection of children's literature and decides on a book about a child who moves to the United States from another country, a book on growing up with two mothers, a book on the power of girls and boys, a book about how family members take care of one another during the Great Depression, and a book about a child who is adopted.

After selecting the books, Aanetra reflects on them carefully. Her first thoughts are on the children in her class who reflect each specific diversity. She will not single them out during the lesson, but wants to be sensitive to their identity and feelings. She will observe them carefully during the lesson to see how they are responding. She asks herself whether the book honors their cultural experiences in a positive and respectful way, or whether the book could make them feel uncomfortable.

Aanetra then considers the impact that the book will have on all of the other children in the class, some of whom may well have bias toward the topic. What preparations should be done before the book is read? What perspective should she carefully articulate before and after she reads it?

Finally, she thinks about how each book will help her emphasize her se-lected theme of *competence within difference*. What are the strengths that she will emphasize? How will she articulate the difference and encourage the chil-dren to find differences interesting? Aanetra decides to develop follow-up activi-ties after listening carefully to what the children say in a discussion after reading each book.

ANTI-BIAS EDUCATION: NAVIGATING THE PARALLEL STREAMS

The field of early childhood education has been greatly influenced by the publication of *Anti-Bias Curriculum: Tools for Empowering Young Chil-dren* (Derman-Sparks & A.B.C. Task Force, 1989). That book enhanced an early shift from a relatively neutral pluralistic approach on appreciat-ing diversity to a focus on social justice and activism for change. As we approach anti-bias education, we support cultural understandings while encouraging an empowered vision of the importance of *activism* in the context of unfairness (Derman-Sparks & Ramsey, 2006). An anti-bias curriculum can help children see and act on injustice in the classroom, and it can further help them see themselves as change-agents as they grow into adulthood.

Many classroom teachers, in my experience, have been oriented more toward multicultural education for cultural understanding than anti-bias education for active resistance to injustice. This may be due to the focus of their teacher preparation programs, but also may reflect a greater comfort with discussing cultural differences than helping children to critique social injustice. Many educators have told me, for example, that they lack confidence in their ability to speak with the children in their classrooms about racism and other forms of social oppression.

In response to the above challenges, I began, some years ago, to introduce multicultural and anti-bias education with the idea of "parallel streams." I emphasized that it is as important to be comfortable with the stream of activism to interrupt oppressions in our classrooms and schools as it is to guide children toward learning about interesting cultural differences. I further indicated that the parallel streams often intersect in our classrooms as we interrupt prejudiced words or discriminatory behaviors and also think about how we can help the children further appreciate the diversities that have emerged as problematic in the classroom. The streams, as I envision them, meet in the "river" of dynamic respect for diversity combined with activism for social change.

Jordan's Project on Farming and Diversity

Jordan has been thinking a lot about ways to focus on the strengths that his 3- to 5-year-olds develop in their rural community. He has completely restructured a differentiated farming project for his children; he wants to honor their cultural experiences while expanding their multicultural and anti-bias knowledge and skills. Specifically, he wants them to be aware of the farming of different products by different people in different places, and wants them to think as activists for the present and future needs of people who farm. Jordan wants to be sure to choose a book and photographs that show a variety of women and men with a variety of skin tones engaged in farming.

Jordan Conceptualizes the Project. The project will start with exploration of farming in the community in which the child-care center is located and then expand to farming in different places. The children will explore differences and similarities in terrains and products, and also will discuss some of the difficulties of farming. They also will plant a small window garden in their classroom and talk about how to be fair in the sharing of opportunities to take care of it.

Toward the end of the project, Jordan will read the children an early-reader book on the work of farming activists Cesar Chavez and Dolores Huerta. In addition, he will arrange for a farmer from the community to come to talk about problems she encounters and ways that activists have helped her. Finally, the children will write a letter or draw a picture to send to a legislator, reflecting challenges of small farmers.

Jordan Makes a Plan. Jordan does research on the problems faced by different farmers in different states. He also will work with the children before the speaker comes to help them to develop questions about the challenges of farming and the ways that people who are activists can help. Jordan also finds pictures of local and state legislators to show the children; he will stress the importance of letting people who are leaders know about the needs and problems of farmers in the community. (All of these activities require differentiation based on the ages and interests of the children.)

CULTURALLY RELEVANT TEACHING

Culturally relevant teaching is a strategy that helps teachers to demonstrate caring connectedness while empowering the intellectual, social, and emotional development of every student (Ladson-Billings, 2009). It has three main characteristics: (1) Teachers have high expectations and encourage academic excellence; (2) teachers help children to develop cultural competence by infusing multiple perspectives, cultures, people, and world-views into their curriculum, and (3) teachers equip children with an understanding of the issues of power, privilege, and oppression, as well as ideas of how they might work for social justice (Castagno, 2009; Ladson-Billings, 1995). Through the lens of culturally responsive teaching, children can experience optimal academic development, develop cultural competence, and begin to understand and critique the issues of power, privilege, and oppression.

Emilio Balances Academic English with a Heritage Project

Emilio's bilingual students will be taking a number of standardized state tests next year. Now that they are in 3rd grade, they are expected to increase their competence in Academic English. The school district has a highly structured curriculum; many of the children in this urban district change their address a number of times during any given year. The goal of the district is to be sure that any new school they attend is at the same point in grade-level curriculum.

Emilio knows that things soon will be changing for his students. In the upper elementary grades their instruction in Spanish will be reduced, and they will be expected to understand and use more Academic English. Further, the stakes will be higher in terms of standardized testing. Emilio has always had the goal of supporting the cultural identities and heritage language of his students; now he is planning a project to span over several months to further reach that goal.

Emilio Conceptualizes His Approach. Emilio studied in college with several professors who emphasized culturally relevant teaching. He recently looked at some old class notes and feels that he could be doing more in that regard. So he decides to make a three-pronged plan that addresses high expectations for success, cultural competence, and critical thinking about the experience of being bilingual.

Emilio Makes a Plan. First of all, Emilio is concerned about the ways many of his students view themselves in terms of academic ability. They sometimes resist difficult tasks or give up on them too easily. He wants his students to enter 4th grade with competence and confidence. While Emilio's expectations for his students are already high, he decides to articulate them more fully on a daily basis. *"Yo quiero que sean exitosos y quiero que sepan que ser exitoso requiere mucho trabajo y esfuerzo. Somos un equipo. Cuando ustedes se esfuerzan yo les enseñaré todas las cosas buenas que han logrado."* ["I want you to be successful and I want you to know that it takes hard work to be successful. We are partners. When you work hard, I will show you all the good things that you have accomplished."]

Emilio is going to use a timer for "work times" and be more insistent on students' full effort for the entire period.

Next, Emilio wants to invite some role models into the classroom. After seeking approval from his principal, he contacts the local Boys and Girls Club to ask about volunteers who are bilingual and have the clearances required by the state. He is given contact numbers for three people, all of whom are able to make a visit to his classroom. Emilio invites them to come during Academic English work time to provide extra support and encouragement for the children. He asks them to stress the value of working hard and to tell the students specific strengths that they notice. After work time, Emilio asks the volunteers to tell the children about their own experiences in learning English and how they benefitted from being bilingual and able to use the languages of their school and community.

Emilio also plans an ongoing project for Friday afternoon flex-time. Up to now, he has been using that time to catch up on subjects or assignments. Emilio is going to talk with the children about their heritage language and how important it is to them. They will each have a small notebook in which to write the story of their heritage language. What do they remember about learning to talk, with whom did they talk, what do they like about their first language? This will be a relaxed assignment, but Emilio will encourage them to write in Spanish and English.

He also plans discussions with the children about how they feel about Spanish in the school—he wants to encourage them to think critically about their experiences. What do they notice about other classrooms where everyone speaks only English? He'll extend his discussions to consider many global languages. Emilio does not want his students to feel isolated; rather, he wants them to see their connection with many people around the world who speak two or more languages. He also wants them to see value in retaining their heritage language while becoming more comfortable and fluent in English.

MULTICULTURAL EDUCATION AND RESISTANCE

A college professor is invited by a superintendent to speak to teachers in his district about multicultural education. The courts have mandated the presentation in partial resolution of a discrimination case against the district. When the professor arrives in the auditorium of the administration building, the superintendent nervously tells her to give the presentation and get off the stage quickly without answering questions. He also informs her that the teachers' union had challenged mandatory attendance at the presentation; the district compromise was that the teachers must be in hearing distance but are not required to be seated in the auditorium. As the professor speaks to the assembled audience, she can see some teachers seated, some teachers standing in the open doorway, and some out in the hall. Many are attentive; some are talking and laughing. There is a small but discernible level of hostility in the response of some of the teachers in the hallway. At the end of her presentation there is some light applause; the administrator and superintendent are very pleased with this and relieved that negative incidents did not take place.

Does the above story surprise you? I was the college professor, and this was far from an isolated experience when I first began to provide multicultural professional development in school districts in the 1980s. Today, multicultural education is better integrated into the mindset of educators, but the fact that there is less open controversy does not mean the absence of resistance. Multicultural education, like all struggles for human rights in any form, can be expected to remain a challenge that is embraced by some and resisted by others.

Why the Continuing Controversy?

Multicultural education is very different from traditional school subjects like mathematics and literacy. Those subjects, while complex, are not fundamentally controversial. New and better methods of teaching continue to emerge, but there is general consensus that the subjects themselves are essential. Multicultural education, on the other hand, emerged from the contested grounds of oppression and legalized discrimination in the United States. Its very existence stems from the abridgment of rights experienced by cultural groups outside of the White European tradition in our democracy. Thus, it is not a call to a comfort zone; it is a call to step forward and make a commitment to fair and equal treatment for all children in the schools of the United States.

Praxis: The Power to Act

Ultimately your intentions as a teacher committed to respect for diversity come down to the idea of "praxis"—real talk and real action. Praxis involves critical thinking, reflection, and analysis of problems; it is linked to actions designed to change the world (Ayers, Kumashiro, Meiners, Quinn, & Stovall, 2010). While praxis is complex idea, it truly can be a part of your everyday life in your classroom. This is because the call to respect diversity is deeply embedded in the call to be a teacher—to deeply influence the lives of others for the better. These words can guide us:

> Every human being is a three-dimensional creature much like yourself—a person with hopes, dreams, skills and experiences; each with a body, mind, and spirit that must somehow be valued, respected, and represented in your classroom and somehow taken into account in your teaching. (Ayers et al., 2010, p. 19)

Teachers should not think about multicultural education, anti-bias education, and culturally responsive teaching as overwhelmingly complicated. They are in many ways a natural extension of learning as much as you possibly can about the lives of your students and using what you learn to teach and build positive relationships (Koppelman, 2011).

Kira Learns About Her Students Through Wall Art

Kira's transitional kindergarten students were very excited about the model of their public housing project in the library. She wants to continue to encourage their sense of culture and identity in the school. Kira has heard some of them say that they were "left back" in kindergarten because they didn't "do good"—they may have heard this from older siblings or children in the lunchroom or on the playground. She is concerned about this and feels that she must find a way to encourage her students. To be better able to do this, Kira decides to try to learn more about their lives and experiences.

Kira Conceptualizes Her Approach. Kira knows her children enjoy art; she decides on a long-term art project that will help her get to know her students better. She searches the teacher supply room and finds a huge, heavy roll of brown paper; the administrative assistant in the office confirms that she is welcome to use it. She has already been collecting crayons and markers from friends and family members whose children have outgrown them. Her plan is to make one wall of her classroom into an "art wall" with space for every child to draw or write during designated times during the day—particularly the brief play periods before school starts and at the end of the day.

Kira Makes a Plan. Kira is going to cover one wall of her classroom with brown paper from the roll every week. She will make the crayons and colored pens she has collected accessible in a covered container. Kira's plan is to provide her students with the daily opportunity to represent their thoughts, feelings, and experiences on the wall art. At the beginning of the project, Kira plans to write the name of every child on the paper, with a designated space for drawing or writing. It will take some time to get the children into the routine; Kira will prepare them carefully. They can choose to draw in their section before school or while they wait for dismissal; Kira will look for other spaces in the day where they might have the freedom to draw. There will not be any requirements; each child can choose when and whether to add something to the wall. She is not sure of exactly how things will go, but she knows that a lot of her students have had enjoyable summer experiences with art and are quite comfortable with self-expression.

At morning meeting at the end of the week, the students will "tour" the wall and will be welcome to speak more about what they have written or drawn. Kira is hoping that she will be learning a lot about her students' lives from the wall—how they see themselves in school and community, what they worry about, the people in their lives, and happy or sad things that happen. She hopes to become more familiar with their cultural experiences and plans to bring them into her teaching as much as possible.

Kira also plans to bring in a picture of a museum painting every week to show the children—she wants them to expand their understanding of art as connected to experience. Ultimately, she wants to interrupt feelings of failure or inferiority and bolster her students' engagement in school by honoring their thoughts, feelings, and experiences in her classroom.

Some Concluding Thoughts on Diversity

Respect for diversity requires constant reflection on the part of teachers. They need to know how their beliefs are affecting the children and how they might benefit the children more. Teachers continually must question their assumptions—"the most treacherous aspect of life in a classroom" (Garcia, 2002, p. 25). It can be very interesting to conceptualize teaching as a subversive activity. Teachers observe to see what their students actually need in order to succeed and then continually seek ways to transcend forces inside and outside of the school that may be negatively affecting their lives (Ladson-Billings, 2009; Postman & Weingartner, 1969).

The aims of multicultural education are the stated aims of the United States—justice and equal treatment for all. Ultimately, we can envision equal treatment as "the infusion of whatever it takes to make things right and to make things fair . . . for the greater good" in the place and time in which we teach (Macdonald, 2011, p. vii).

SOME PRACTICAL IDEAS FOR GETTING STARTED

Many teachers are feeling pressured to teach academic subjects to young children. Some might think or say, "I don't have time during the day for multicultural education." It is very important to move away from that mindset. I would argue that multicultural education *is your day.* It is the way you approach the children, design instruction, think about content, talk with your students, interpret their words and actions, and seek to make their lives better. Multicultural education is not something extra—it is the heart of what you do and seek as a teacher.

Think About Your Own Life Story

You may have written autobiographies in a former multicultural course or in other stages of your education. This is a good time to think your life story through again. How did you learn about yourself through others? How did you learn and come to think about people different from yourself? What were the positive experiences that helped you to develop into someone who has dedicated his or her life to teaching others? What were the experiences that created bias toward others? How and why did you start to question that bias? You have an interesting past; think back so it can further guide you into self-understanding and awareness of others.

Think More About the Diversities in Your Life

How have you been thinking about diversity up to now? What would you say are the major diversities in your life? This might depend on your own culture and ethnicity and the place where you live as well as your classroom. In your social activities and experiences, who tends to be included or excluded?

It is possible that you will realize it is time to seek out different kinds of diversity. Possibly you might attend a lecture or event focused on a culture about which you know very little, or speak more to someone you know whose cultural experiences are very different from your own. It can be a good idea to read a book written by someone with whom you routinely disagree or regard with some suspicion. What does that person have to say, and how might you better understand that perspective? The more you open your own mind to different people and experiences, the better able you will be to help your students to be culturally competent.

Acknowledge Prejudice When You See or Hear It

"She is amazing! She grew up in a trailer camp with a single mother and five siblings and got all the way to an Ivy League college!"

"You might want to consider taking a look at the public school in our community; some of my friends who at first wouldn't even consider sending their child to public school have been very happy with it."

"Considering the kind of children who come to this program, I have a fairly bright and nice group this year."

Critical listening teaches us a lot about assumptions about diversity. What forces in our society make it "amazing" for someone who grew up outside of affluence to go to an elite school? What is it about that particular public school that makes it more feasible for people inclined to use private schools to send their children to? Is that comment code for "only White children attend" or "everyone in the school is affluent"? What cultural characteristics does "the kind of children" have, and why is being "bright and nice" considered to be unexpected? Seemingly benign statements can carry heavy bias. When we acknowledge that bias, even silently to ourselves, we are becoming better able to think critically about diversity in our society and our classrooms.

Follow the Teacher-Guides

In this chapter, our teacher-guides incorporated multicultural, anti-bias, and culturally responsive practices in their classrooms. *These did not come from prepackaged curriculum; rather they emerged from the teachers' knowledge of and care about their students.* The teachers each found a way to use the lives and cultural experiences of their students to expand their understanding of self and others.

Further, their strategies increased their students' ability to see themselves as capable learners and critical thinkers. Our teacher-guides saw themselves as empowered within the confines of their sites of practice—thus they were able to seek greater empowerment for their students. Each teacher demonstrated the kind of respect for diversity that ultimately can give children a sense of belief in their own power to think critically and to have an impact on the world.

Questions for Discussion

1. How would you describe your own background and experiences in the areas of multicultural, anti-bias, and culturally relevant teaching? Do you feel well prepared, or do you acknowledge your need to think and learn more about these approaches?
2. How might you describe the areas of prejudice, discrimination, or bias that influenced you when you were growing up? Did you experience them yourself? Did you feel that you had a sense of privilege or a right to look down on certain other children?
3. What are some strategies that you use, or plan to use, to get to know your students better from a cultural perspective? How will you suspend assumptions and adopt a sense of inquiry?
4. What are some ways in which you might evaluate multicultural curriculum before using it with children?
5. How would you describe your specific intentions in terms of integrating respect for diversity into your daily life as a teacher?

Four

Dynamic Ethics in the Lives of Early Childhood Teachers

Reflection on the subject of ethics provides teachers with the opportunity to reconsider the quality of their character and the strength of moral compass that guides them through daily life. Ethics are deeply embedded in our personal as well as our professional lives; in both realms they have a powerful effect on everyone around us. Ethical principles do not exist in a comfort zone; we must always question a sense of confidence that we are living in a good and just way. We seek to be moral and ethical throughout our lives by reflecting continually and seriously on our personal and professional actions.

DEFINING ETHICS AND MORALITY IN THE EVERYDAY

The subject of ethics is the branch of philosophy that formulates questions concerning the ways in which people should be expected to act toward one another (Durac, 2011). To be ethical is to be attentive to guiding principles and to be able to explain and justify the actions that we take in light of them (Taggart, 2011). As Feeney and Freeman (2005) indicate, "Ethics is the study of right and wrong, duty and obligations. It involves critical reflection on morality. Many call ethics the science of moral duty" (p. 5).

Ethics are far more a matter of *questioning ourselves* than assuring others of the rightness of our action. We would not say, "I am being ethical," as much as, "I wonder whether this is the ethical response to this situation." To seek to be ethical is to *wonder* whether we are taking the right action in responding to a situation, and to consider a number of alternatives before making a decision.

An Ethical Question

Let's say, for example, that a child in your classroom is exhibiting difficult behaviors. She pushes and hits other children, and is defiant when asked to clean up at the end of play time. You spoke with her mother about her behavior on the phone earlier in the year; the little girl came to school the next day with welts on her hands. When you asked about them, she said her mother had hit her because she was "bad in school." When you shared your concern about this with the director, she was supportive but indicated that hitting children on their hands was considered standard child discipline in the culture of the community. You were not comfortable with this but decided to focus on continuing to try to help the child improve her behavior. Now, although you think her mother needs to know that her child's behavior has not improved, you wonder whether calling the home is the right thing to do.

This is an *ethical* question because it is a question of right and wrong. The solution is complex and must be considered carefully. Should you consult with your director before making a decision? Is it better to just try as hard as possible to help the child improve her behavior without calling the mother? Does her mother have a right to know how she is acting? We will return to these questions a bit later in the chapter when we further consider the Code of Ethics of the National Association for the Education of Young Children (NAEYC, 2011).

Ethics and Personal Qualities

While the field of ethics is often associated with codes and principles, it also draws on personal qualities such as care, patience, persistence, and courage (Taggart, 2011). Ethical personal qualities are reflected in eight general principles: (1) respecting the autonomy of others, (2) doing no harm, (3) being of benefit to others, (4) valuing fairness and equity, (5) exhibiting fidelity and honesty, (6) affording dignity to all others, (7) caring about others, and (8) doing one's best in all situations (Keith-Spiegel, Whitley, Balogh, Perkins, & Whittig, 2002). These principles do not exist in the realm of the abstract; the ethical person must enact them in personal and professional life.

Ethics and Moral Character

Ethics require us to consciously adhere to high standards of morality and virtue. It is never enough to claim that our standards are high; we need to make moral decisions in complex situations that *demonstrate* our standards (Johns, McGrath, & Mather, 2008). Moral issues do not exist in a vacuum—they "concern our duties and obligations to one another" (p. 4) as we consider the human rights that dictate fair treatment of those with whom we are in contact (Strike & Soltis, 2004).

Teaching is a moral endeavor. Teaching is far more than the utilization of pedagogical technique; it is a moral endeavor as well. Teachers continually must consider issues of right and wrong in every aspect of their practice (Sockett, 1993). Our consideration of moral issues should always be evident in our discourse concerning resolution of problems related to practice.

Consider, for example, a hypothetical conversation between two kindergarten teachers who are taking their classes on a fieldtrip in a few days. They are discussing a child who recently has entered a foster home and has not returned a permission slip. An *expedient* statement might be:

> "We sent the slip home to all families last week and tried to reach those who did not return it. The foster mother did not return our call. We have done what we could—this child will have to stay at school in another classroom during the trip."

On the other hand, a statement that reflects *moral* considerations might be:

> "We sent all of the families the slip and tried to call all the parents who did not return them. I am concerned that we never got a response from the foster mother. But, is it right to disappoint this child? She has already been upset by her removal from her home; I fear that she will feel very hurt if excluded. Maybe one of us could give her social worker a call from the school office and ask if he could contact her new foster mother concerning the permission slip, so we might get it by tomorrow."

Constructing an ethical reputation. When we talk openly and regularly about *rightness* of decisions that affect others, we can build a personal reputation for moral integrity. Ultimately, such a reputation has a profound influence on the learning, teaching, and effectiveness of others (Palmer, 2007). Having that reputation also helps us as teachers to continually reflect more carefully on what we say and do. This is because we can be absolutely sure that those with whom we speak about what is right or wrong are going to look closely at us to judge evidence of our own integrity. This provides us with the motivation to continue to conduct ourselves in the ways that we would recommend for others (Sockett, 1993).

FIRST DO NO HARM

The first and most important principle in codes of ethics for teachers is that children should not be harmed in the process of education. The

NAEYC Code of Ethical Conduct and Statement of Commitment (2011) makes this clear in the first principle of the statement of Ethical Responsibilities to Children:

> Above all, we shall not harm children. We shall not participate in practices that are emotionally damaging, physically harmful, disrespectful, degrading, dangerous, exploitative, or intimidating to children. *This principle has precedence over all others in this Code.*

While ethics can at times seem confusing and abstract, this first principle is one we should keep in mind every single day of our careers. Every action we take as teachers, even corrective actions, must reflect respect, compassion, and concern for positive child development.

Kira Resolves an Ethical Dilemma with the Librarian

Kira has been feeling very positive about her efforts to get to know her transitional kindergarten students and to represent them respectfully to other faculty members in the school. However, she remains aware of some of the ways in which some teachers continue to view them as deficient—not as good as the other kindergarten children in the building.

Kira has started to wonder whether the school librarian is being negative and disapproving with her students during storytime. The past few times her students returned from their weekly library hour, they seemed to be somewhat downhearted. This week they returned to her room upset; several of the students were crying. One of the students gave her a note written by the librarian indicating that their behavior had been unacceptable.

When Kira asked her students what happened in the library, they indicated that two of their classmates had broken the rule of silence as they entered the library. After they were all seated, the librarian indicated anger about the misbehavior. As punishment, they were told that the story would not be read and they would have to sit in silence for the entire period. This was especially hard for the children because, the week before, the librarian had promised to read a seasonal book on this day. They had all been looking forward to the story and were deeply disappointed.

Kira felt very angry. Up to now she had avoided confrontation with other teachers, but today this treatment seemed to be harmful and completely unfair. Why were all the children denied a story they had been promised because two of them apparently engaged in minor misbehavior as they entered the room? As a first-year teacher, she has worked hard to avoid confrontational actions with others in the building. But today, after seeing her class upset and crying, she feels that she must take action and do something to stand up for her students.

Taking her copy of the NAEYC Code of Ethics out of her desk drawer, she rereads the first principle, P-1.1, "Above all, we shall not harm children" (p. 3). She also reads principle P-1.2, "We shall care for and educate children in positive emotional and social environments . . . ," and principle P-1.3, "We shall not participate in practices that discriminate against children by denying benefits . . ." (p. 3). This convinces Kira that she has encountered an ethical dilemma that must be addressed.

As she thinks about things more, Kira reminds herself that she has heard only one interpretation of the events in the library—that of her young students. Turning to the section on Ethical Responsibilities to Colleagues, she takes note of principle P-3A-2, "When we have concerns about the professional behavior of a co-worker, we shall first let that person know of our concern in a way that shows respect for personal dignity . . ." (p. 5). Kira realizes now that it is her responsibility to ask the librarian about the note she sent back to the classroom with the students. This undoubtedly will shed some light on what took place, and the librarian might have an entirely different perspective on the course of events.

When she calms down a bit, Kira decides to ask the librarian whether they might meet during morning planning time the next day to discuss the note she sent back with the children. Kira plans to listen respectfully to the concerns of the librarian and to ask about what happened regarding the children and the book to be read that day. Kira also plans to make herself clear in a nice and professional way; she does not agree that a whole class should be denied their library hour because two children misbehaved. Her suggestion, considering the age of the children, would be a mild reprimand or warning for those children having a brief conversation while entering the library. Kira hopes that the discussion will go well; after evaluating the outcome of the initial meeting, she will make a decision about asking the principal to meet with her and the library teacher.

What do you think about Kira's plan? Should she instead go right to the principal with a complaint? Should she seek advice from other teachers first? As a first-year teacher, is it wise for her to create a possible conflict with the library teacher? What other approaches might she consider? Since questions are an integral part of ethical deliberation, I have altered the question format for this chapter in a different way. Rather than place them at the end, I have included questions after each of our hypothetical teacher-guides resolves an ethical issue. Think about points of agreement and disagreement. What might you add if you were part of a group discussion of each of the ethical dilemmas?

Many teachers remain silent in ethical conflict because they are unsure of what to do. In this case, the NAEYC Code appears to support Kira's concern and to provide direction in terms of an appropriate response. However, it is important to reiterate that ethical decisions always involve questions. Is Kira risking her future relationship with the librarian? Would a damaged professional relationship have further repercussions for her students? Kira, in this case, is willing to take some risks because she truly feels that what happened in the library was harmful. She seeks to treat all persons with respect in her personal life, and she has stood up in the past for people in her family and community who she felt had been treated unfairly. Kira feels that she has a moral as well as a professional obligation to speak up about the library incident.

ETHICS IN OUR PERSONAL LIVES

The first step in reflecting on personal ethics is to ask, "How should I live my life?" The answer varies from person to person, but in general the ethical life will be conducted in a way that expresses our desire to do what is right and to bring no intentional harm to others. The central focus of ethics is social: How do we treat other people?

In the theory of ethics formulated by Russian philosopher Mikhail Bakhtin, we are always required to consider our moral obligation to others in the way in which we live. He believed that we are all responsible for our desires, our words, and our deeds, and must consider their impact on those with whom we live and work. To Bakhtin, every moment of life involves a choice of response for which we are responsible; he believed that no one had the right to abdicate that responsibility (Pollard, 2011).

Connection of Personal to Professional

There is a close connection between personal and professional ethics. For example, the teacher who strives diligently to be fair, responsible, and trustworthy with her family and in her community is very likely to also consider those virtues important in her professional work. Conversely, the teacher who behaves in a dishonest and unreliable manner with her family and in her community is likely to demonstrate similar behaviors in the professional setting (Campbell, 2003). Today, our personal lives rarely are completely private; inevitably, some of our professional peers, family members, and community members are aware of our strength of character or lack thereof. It is therefore essential for teachers to work hard to maintain a consistently high standard of ethical integrity in their personal as well as their professional lives (Haydon, 2006). A lack of coherence between how we are known to act in the private sector and what we profess to value as professionals may result in a judgment of hypocrisy and loss of professional credibility.

Faith Traditions

It is important to establish some essential differences between values held by our faith traditions and our adherence to professional values and ethics. As citizens we have freedom of religion; educators who follow a faith tradition may hold a variety of beliefs about right and wrong in areas such as human sexuality, dietary practices, clothing, and gender roles. The U.S. Constitution protects our right to chosen beliefs, but we must always keep in mind that it protects the freedoms and rights of all others as well (Murray, 2008).

As teachers who hold the public trust, we have the duty to understand and respect the perspectives of multiple religious beliefs. For example, possibly our own faith tradition does not accept divorce, homosexuality, or the birth of children outside of marriage. As citizens, whatever our faith-based beliefs may be, we have the obligation to acknowledge the legally protected rights of others to make decisions, act in their own best interest, and establish their own sexual identities. Further, as ethical professionals, we may not allow our personal faith-based beliefs to interfere with our adherence to the core value of the NAEYC Code of Ethical Conduct and Statement of Commitment that we "respect the dignity, worth, and uniqueness of each individual (child, family member, and colleague)" (2011, p. 1).

Emilio Seeks an Ethical Stance on Homosexuality

Emilio has been very pleased with his efforts to build acceptance of his bilingual students in his school. The teachers with whom he formed a coalition have continued to put Spanish and English words on their hallway bulletin boards, and they feel that they have had some success in addressing deficit-based comments about students in the school with the plan of action that they developed in Chapter 2 around the use of language.

Because Emilio sees himself as an activist, he has been unsettled by his discomfort with the gay relationship of the father of a girl in his class this year. When he overhears this girl being teased on the playground with some taunts about men who are gay, he finds himself uncharacteristically hesitant to interfere. Emilio does walk over and interrupt the children who are involved and says that it is wrong to be unkind to others. However, he finds himself unsure of what to say to them and to his student about the specific "gay" taunts. Emilio recognizes the need to reflect on his attitudes and to respond to the situation as ethically as possible.

Emilio has retained the faith tradition with which he was raised; in his church and his family, homosexuality is considered unacceptable. Growing up, when his cousins and friends made fun of people who were gay or lesbian, he often would join them. Although his teacher education program had a strong anti-bias orientation, he now realizes that he never adopted a positive attitude toward relational preferences. Homosexuality has continued to make him uncomfortable.

Consulting the NAEYC Code of Ethics, he reads the "Ideals" in the section on Ethical Responsibilities to Families. One (I-2.5) indicates that he is expected to "respect the dignity and preferences of each family . . ." and another (I-2.4) that he is "to listen to families, acknowledge and build upon their strengths and competencies, and learn from families . . ." (p. 4). Emilio is still unsure about what to do. He talks with a teacher with whom he is friendly and whose daughter is married to a woman in a nearby state. His friend suggests that he talk privately with the girl in his class to offer her support. Emilio, he further suggests, should maintain an accepting and natural tone during the conversation, indicating that he is sorry the children acted so unkindly toward her.

Emilio decides to take this advice and plans to leave open spaces in the conversation for the girl to possibly share more about her family life with her father and his partner. He plans to be supportive, acknowledging that many people in the United States are in same-sex relationships or marriages . . . no one has the right to be disrespectful toward them. *"En el mundo existen diferentes tipos de parejas y relaciones. Se quieren y se cuidan y eso es bueno. Es injusto que te molesten o hieran por la relación de tu papá."* ["People live in different kinds of relationships. They love and care for each other, which is good. It is unfair for anyone to tease or hurt you because of your father's relationship."]

Emilio is also determined to make the most of the next parent meeting with the father and his partner, and to actively address any further incidents among students that reflect anti-gay bias.

What do you think of Emilio's decisions? Do you think he has done too much or too little? Do you see a conflict between his faith tradition and his adherence to the code of ethics? Clearly, Emilio is still growing into his personal stance on sexual orientation. However, his consultation of the code has supported reflection and change on his part.

EMBRACING A PROFESSIONAL CODE OF ETHICS

A professional code of ethics provides support for equal and fair consideration of the rights of others. It moves us beyond personal opinion or "value judgments" into a sophisticated sphere of specified commitments and expectations. While a great deal of interpretation is always involved in complex ethical reasoning, professional codes provide strong and consistent guidance.

Our personal values tend to be culturally based and reflective of the experiences we have had throughout our lives. Professional ethics, on the other hand, "concern the kinds of actions that are right and wrong in the workplace and are a public matter" (Feeney & Freeman, 2005, p. 6). All early childhood educators have the responsibility to focus on the ethical environment of their workplace (Haydon, 2006). This means that they must make daily moral judgments based on existing guidelines that clarify their professional duties as well as what they "ought to do and ought not to do" (Strike & Soltis, 2004, p. 7).

The NAEYC Code

The NAEYC Code of Ethical Conduct and Statement of Commitment (2011) also is endorsed by the Association for Childhood Education International and the National Association for Family Child Care. It serves as a detailed position statement of ethical expectations for all who work with young children. This Code is easily accessed from the Internet and is nine pages in length. All early childhood programs as well as early childhood educators should have the Code readily available for daily consultation as necessary.

The NAEYC Code of Ethics gives early childhood educators a strong sense of professional identity as it reinforces the knowledge, dispositions, and skills that promote sound judgments of right and wrong (Giovacco-Johnson, 2011). It identifies two vital aspects of ethical behavior in early childhood education—knowing and acting on the core ideals of the profession, and knowing and using the Code in daily practice (Feeney & Freeman, 2005). The four sections of the Code address professional relationships with children, with families, among colleagues, and with the community and society, through identification of ideals and principles for practice.

Using the Code

The ethical decisionmaking process generally involves sensitivity to a problem, interpretation of the situation, reasoning to determine a course of action, and action with clear intention (Durac, 2011). Stephanie Feeney and Nancy Freeman, in their book *Ethics and the Early Childhood Educator: Using the NAEYC Code* (2005), provide a detailed map through which teachers can work while making decisions about an ethical dilemma (p. 25). For example, the educator is assisted in deciding whether the problem is indeed one of ethics (concerning issues of right or wrong) and in making a decision on a course of action (Is it best for the community and the profession? Does it treat people and relationships with respect?). Consultation with the NAEYC Code is recommended as a guide in prioritizing values as the ethical problem is addressed.

Let's return to the little girl with the challenging behavior that we met earlier in this chapter. Her mother responded to the former phone call of the teacher by hitting the child on her hands for misbehavior. The teacher is now weighing the decision of whether to inform the mother that the problems have not been alleviated. She does not want to wrong the child by exposing her to punishment at home that may not alleviate the problem at school; she seeks the right action in terms of the best way to support the positive development of the child.

After a careful examination of the section on Ethical Responsibilities to Children, she settles on Principle P-1.4, which encourages two-way communications that include other staff and the family in making a decision regarding a child. Thus, she decides that her first step will be to consult with her director and suggest a three-way meeting with the mother. Her hope is that the mother can be better helped to understand the developmental issues faced by her child and that the three of them might collaborate on a proactive plan that involves encouragement and possibly some rewards.

NEGOTIATING THE CODE WITH OTHERS

Since ethics as a field is social in nature, our ethical decisions often must involve collaboration with others. Hopefully, the Code has helped us to develop a professional community that is maintaining agreed-upon standards and commitments (Sockett, 1993). Even so, the very nature of the questioning that is essential to the practice of ethical consideration virtually ensures multiple perspectives and even disagreements about appropriate ethical responses to some situations.

Habermas and Communal Ethics

German philosopher Jurgen Habermas theorized that moral norms must always be arrived upon through intersubjective dialogue—he did not believe it was possible for individuals to establish them alone (Head, 2008). In his idea of "communicative democracy" (p. 11) Habermas suggested that members of a community come together voluntarily to justify decisions through arguments, explanations, and different modes of persuasion (Zajda et al., 2006). Ultimately, Habermas urged the formation of consensus based on comprehensibility, truth, rightness, and sincerity (Head, 2008).

Participatory Advocacy in Ethics Discourse

The theory of Habermas, while valuable, may assume a more sophisticated level of collaborative discourse than exists in many educational settings. Some institutions may be better characterized by quiet behind-the-scenes talk about controversial issues than by open discourse about matters of ethics (Campbell, 2003). An important goal in that situation, according to Habermas, would be the construction of a stronger community of open discourse.

Could your school community benefit from stronger opportunities for better ethical communication? If so, this is a good time to think back to the discussion of *participatory advocacy* in Chapter 1—the advocacy related to active engagement in open school discourse. If your site of practice is characterized by ethical issues that are silenced, discussed by only a few, or even ignored, you as an advocate might decide to seek opportunities to encourage and engage in open discussion of moral or ethical matters in the school setting.

Jordan Applies Ethics to Talk About a Colleague

Jordan has enjoyed his efforts to support identity and critical thinking in his rural students. He and other teachers are continuing to jot down strengths they notice in the children on the large sheets of paper posted in the faculty room. In the past few months, however, a new problem has emerged in the center.

A new faculty member was hired for the other 3–5-year-olds in the class this year: a young woman from another state whose husband is doing doctoral work at the university where Jordan currently is getting his graduate degree. The new teacher has not been socially well accepted in the center. She seems cold and unfriendly, and keeps to herself; she also has been outspoken in criticizing some of the policies and practices in the center. A small group of female teachers seems to have banded together to complain about the new teacher.

Privately, Jordan agrees that the new teacher has been unfriendly; at times he feels that she looks down on the center as necessary temporary employment. Yet, he also has seen a lot of strengths and talent in her. She knows a great deal about child development and has infused a lot of art and dance into her daily curriculum. The children seem to like her quite a bit.

One day, he sees a few parents speaking with some of the teachers who have been complaining about his new colleague. It appears that the parents are claiming that she has made some insulting comments to them about their children. This problem is raised at a faculty meeting at which the new teacher is not present. The director is always open to topics raised by teachers; Jordan is surprised, however, that the claims of the parents appear to be taken by his colleagues at face value.

Jordan tends to play a leadership role in most faculty discussions and he does so in an assertive but friendly and positive manner. He leaves the meeting briefly and returns with the NAEYC Code. "Listen," he says, "we need to be ethical in this conversation. In terms of responsibilities to coworkers (P-3A.I, P-A.3; p. 5), we are required to recognize her contributions, and exercise care in the discussion of her conduct. Not one person here was a witness to the statements she supposedly made, and only a few of us actually spoke with the parents. Let's be fair!"

The director then spoke and reminded the faculty that the new teacher was the first to join the center from outside the community in many years. Possibly, she suggests, they should be open to some differences. She indicates that she will think further about the matter, but also urges the faculty to be welcoming, to see the strengths of the new teacher, to refrain from judgment, and to further refrain from discussions with parents about other teachers in the center.

Gossip and School Climate

What do you think of Jordan's decision to use the NAEYC Code to defend the teacher? Do you think he was more likely to do this as a male? Was it better received by others because he was male? How might you expect to be treated by colleagues if you did the same thing? What do you think of the director's response? Should the discussion have taken place when the new faculty member was not present? The code requires teachers to treat one another with respect and fairness. If a school or program has teacher factions or "cliques," there may be some violations of the code of ethics. As a participatory advocate, how might you help to create a stronger and more ethical school community?

Ethics of Collaborative Discourse

There is a great deal of moral ambiguity in the consideration of ethics; the field of ethics is not as conclusive as subjects such as mathematics. People will disagree (Strike & Soltis, 2004). Also, ethics often involve situations in which no option is completely satisfying and possible steps may seem contradictory or incompatible (Durac, 2011). Thus it must be realized that collaborative discourse about ethical matters will not be a "quick fix." Patient discourse about ethical problems, however, ultimately can lead to well-founded solutions and construct a climate of ethical integrity in the school setting.

The "ground rules" of collaborative discourse might include careful listening, respectful posing of different perspectives, group use of the

NAEYC Code to weigh possible solutions, and clear focus on the good of the students rather than "winners or losers" of ethical arguments.

Ethical Finesse

Many ethical problems can be resolved without conflict through the application of what is called *ethical finesse*. Ethical finesse enables those in deliberation to find the way to solve a problem without an unnecessarily complex value conflict (Feeney & Freeman, 2005). For example, imagine that several children who are Jehovah's Witnesses have been enrolled recently in an early childhood program. This has resulted in the need for ethical rethinking of traditional Christmas-related activities such as parties and tree decorations in the classrooms.

In the process of a related discussion in a faculty meeting, several teachers indicate that they have already been questioning the appropriateness of the program focus on Christmas, which often includes discussion of gifts and Santa Claus. Many of the families lack the resources to have traditional celebrations of Christmas. The teachers consider these points carefully and are able to come to consensus quickly; the program should change to a December theme of the beautiful trees in the community in the coming winter environment. Each class will develop a project based on trees in the cold and snow to display in the hallways of the school toward the end of the month.

To be ethical is to be comfortable with important questions that guide right actions. Over time, our decisions are consistently based in our desire to be ethical by attentiveness, intuition, improvisation, and the experience of trial and error (Pollard, 2011).

BALANCING THE REAL AND IDEAL

Most educators begin their careers with an idealistic vision of success in their future classrooms. While time and experience may temper our expectations, it is important to make an effort to retain our ideals. They can continue to serve as sustaining guides, even when they appear to be unattainable (Sockett, 1993). When we seek an ideal, no matter how elusive, we are more resilient and less likely to give up on our most difficult problems.

Many teachers in my graduate classes over the years have described children in their classrooms who seem to be facing almost insurmountable problems. There are stories of abuse, addiction, arrest, death, abandonment—combinations of unfortunate circumstances that in some cases seem to defy hope. Teachers might share such stories of these children and then ask, "What can anyone really do in a situation like this?" My answer is, "Something can always be done!" (Fennimore, 2007).

We should never think that the only two options available to us as teachers when our students seem to be in terrible circumstances are to either completely resolve the problem or give up on it! There is some action, some expression of care, or some movement in the right direction available to us in any challenging circumstance. And, even if we ultimately feel that our efforts to solve a problem were unsuccessful, we can continue as ethical educators to be concerned and determined to seek future solutions (Noddings, 2005).

Aanetra's Ethical Approach to a Community Issue

Aanetra is enjoying her year in the federally funded preschool program. She feels confident that some progress has been made in building a community of learners in her classroom; she is observing more friendly and caring interactions among all of the children as the year goes on. The family members and caregivers also seem to be chatting more freely with one another at drop-off and pick-up times.

However, a small group of the more affluent parents are starting to be outspoken in their concern that the curriculum does not contain more of an emphasis on academic subjects. They have been pressuring the principal to separate the children into learning groups so their "more advanced" children can focus on math and reading skills. The principal asks Aanetra and her program supervisor to attend a meeting in which they might discuss this parental request.

Aanetra is not comfortable with being outspoken, but she expresses herself clearly. The program is designed to promote social, cognitive, emotional, and physical development in an inclusive environment. Further, it has the philosophy of play-based developmentally appropriate practice. Her program supervisor is somewhat ambivalent; he feels that it is important to retain the presence of the more affluent parents and to acknowledge that some of the children are more advanced than others. Aanetra continues to assert herself—she asks what will happen to the inclusive environment if this kind of grouping is allowed. And will the separation and exposure to early academics really be helpful for the more affluent children?

Ultimately, Aanetra refers to the NAEYC Code on Ethical Responsibilities to Community and Society. Specifically she points out Ideal 1-4.6: "To work toward greater societal acknowledgment of children's rights and greater social acceptance of responsibility for the well-being of all children" (p. 6). She offers to conduct another parent workshop on the importance of a balanced and play-based preschool curriculum. She fully agrees, however, with the suggestion of her supervisor that they examine the curriculum to create more opportunities for differentiated learning for all the children whenever possible.

Ethics and School Politics

What do you think of Aanetra's assertiveness in this matter? Was she fair to parents who wanted their children to have more structured academics in small groups? How should teachers respond when the more privileged and affluent parents express concern about their children's advanced needs in preschool?

Teachers can and should focus their ethical concerns on all available knowledge about the best context for inclusive learning for young children. All children need the opportunity to reach their highest potential within classroom communities that promote fairness, collaboration, and multiple opportunities for learning.

What About Teacher Work Ethic?

A challenge for many teachers is their perception of different levels of work ethic in their colleagues. It may appear that some teachers do the minimum while others are always willing to go the extra mile. Dedicated teachers may become disillusioned or demoralized when they see that the extra efforts they are making to enhance the school and the education of the children are neither recognized nor compensated. It can be difficult for newly hired teachers to accept that those with seniority appear to be doing less and making much higher salaries.

How might one approach this dilemma in an ethical manner? Let's say, for example, that you are an early childhood teacher in a school district in which teachers have a contractual right to leave at 3:10 P.M. Most of the parents have jobs that make it impossible for them to attend meetings with teachers until after 4:00 P.M. When approached by the school administration and asked to stay later for a meeting with a parent, you always agree. It is your ethical position that it would be wrong not to stay because a child or family might be harmed if they do not receive needed assistance. However, the majority of the teachers in your district refuse to do this. As professionals, they believe that it is wrong for the district to ask that they perform uncompensated services beyond their contractual responsibilities.

Conflicted by this situation, you think it through with *reflective questioning*. Are the teachers who refuse to stay violating their contracts or school policies? In this case, they are not. Even so, considering the needs of the parents and children, should their ethics be questioned? Or, rather, is the school district in ethical violation for failing to provide extra compensation for professionals who are meeting the needs of parents and families beyond those required in the contract?

Your questions in this matter probably will fail to produce a clear-cut answer about ethics; the situation is multifaceted and ambiguous. It is probably not helpful to focus on critical thoughts about colleagues. However, you do have the power and responsibility to determine your *own sense of ethical obligation to the parents*. If you believe that it is right to stay after school for a reasonable period of time to address an important issue with a parent, you should do so. Your actions will assist the parents and their children, and you will be making a good and rightful contribution to their well-being.

Further, you may have a positive effect on your colleagues as you lead by example. It is possible that your actions will cause others to reconsider their positions and to remain for meetings when necessary. Also, you might join with others to advocate for the parents with district administrators. Remember that, in any ethical dilemma, you can identify steps that you can take yourself as well as steps that you might take with others to enhance the ethical climate of your school or program.

ETHICS AS APPLIED SOCIAL JUSTICE

It should be clear that *all* early childhood educators are responsible for adherence to their professional code of ethics. Personal values and beliefs, including faith traditions and political positions, may not impinge on their responsibilities. They are charged with the obligation to *do no harm* to children and families and to respect and honor the needs of all individuals in the school or program setting. A profound respect for diversity is deeply embedded in the NAEYC Code; there are no exceptions to the dictate that all must be honored and harm must come to none.

It is for this reason that I believe our NAEYC Code of Ethics and social justice commitments in teacher preparation and practice are inextricably linked. Any abridgment of human rights or discriminatory act in the school or classroom is a violation of the code. Students may enter teacher preparation programs with bias that comes from their family and community experiences. It is not only important but necessary for their programs to teach them how to bridge their personal experiences and beliefs about others to the future necessity that they give equal honor and respect to every child and family in their sites of practice.

SOME PRACTICAL IDEAS FOR GETTING STARTED

Ethics are essential to your construction of an outstanding career in early childhood education. Depending on the current role of the NAEYC Code in your school or program, the following suggestions may be helpful.

Make the Code Available in Your Classroom

Place the code in a desk drawer or in some other easily accessible place, and consult it whenever you think an ethical question might exist. It also can be helpful to take it out when other teachers come to your classroom to discuss issues or problems with children, families, administrators, or colleagues.

This will help you take an ethical approach to the discussion and make the code a natural part of the solution to questions or difficulties in the daily life of the school.

Think About Different Levels of Ethical Problems

There are many ethical questions that can be resolved quickly with finesse. Often, for example, a brief conversation with a colleague, if a question has arisen, will shed light on the problem and lead to positive resolution. However, there are times when the code is necessary to guide more difficult problems on which colleagues have multiple perspectives. On the most difficult level, if you witness or suspect a very serious ethical violation (such as teacher violence or cruelty toward children), you may need to bring the problem to the immediate attention of the school or program administration. Making ethical thinking part of your daily life as a teacher will help you to recognize levels of seriousness and make careful decisions.

FIVE

Commitment in Action
Addressing School Readiness

This chapter is focused on the issue of school readiness, which provides an opportunity to see how information in previous chapters might be applied in the classroom and school setting. It is written from the perspective that every child of school age in the United States is *ready* for school and that schools have the obligation to be *ready for them*. Any assessment of children upon school entry should foster greater understanding of their skills and needs as well as responsible planning to meet their best interests. This is in direct contrast to assessments that judge children, deem them "unready," and assign them to deficit-based school placements. I believe that issues of ethics, justice, respect for diversity, and advocacy potentially arise due to the high expectations that are set for children before their schooling has even begun. All children should have a fair chance to grow and develop in a school-based context of encouragement, support, and high expectations. My graduate students so often ask, "How can we really apply idealistic ideas about teachers as activists in our daily school lives?" This chapter will explore, through the lens of school readiness, the ways in which every early childhood educator can implement advocacy, ethics, commitment to social justice, and respect for diversity in their classrooms and schools in the complex context of the ways in which the concept of "readiness" is implemented in school.

WELCOMING ALL CHILDREN WITH RESPECT AND HIGH REGARD

Simply put, children deserve to be welcomed into schools and provided with the opportunity to learn and grow in optimal educational environments. Within those environments, they need a fair chance to show us who they are and the *capabilities* that they possess. Essential to this process is support and care from teachers who understand and respect their family and cultural experiences.

Children Diagnosed with Disabilities

Many children come to school with identified disabilities; others will be diagnosed with disabilities during their initial years in school. These children have a right to all appropriate supports and protections as provided by federal, state, and school district policies. While special placements or additional resources may be necessary, the disability should be viewed as a *difference* that is welcome in the classroom. The school is responsible for recognizing and utilizing the skills, experiences, and competencies of children with disabilities. Further, all school people are responsible for welcoming the children and including them as valued members of the school and classroom community (Ferri & Bacon, 2011).

Moving away from ableism. The emergence of the field of child development, from its inception, sought to establish universal stages of normal growth and maturation. Children whose disabilities placed them outside of this norm were considered pathological and deficient. This has led to the problem of ableism—of the social belief that one way of developing, or experiencing life, or speaking, or writing, or moving one's body, is better than another (Ferri & Bacon, 2011). Thus, we might hear children with disabilities discussed as having something "wrong with them," while children presumed to be normal are discussed in positive terms. Thinking of children only in terms of their disabilities devalues and excludes them from any normative sense of belonging. They become completely defined by the characteristic that society finds to be deficient.

Moving away from normative thinking. Law professor Kenji Yoshino has suggested in his book *Covering* (2006) that we as a society should start to move away from our current conceptualizations of *normal*. Norms tend to create insiders and outsiders rather than an ethic of belonging that acknowledges universal differences and supports a sense of completeness in all people. We as teachers must be ready to challenge the traditional constructs of disability and normalcy (Ferri & Bacon, 2011). This is a natural extension of respect for diversity. When children come to us with special needs—whether they are identified or not—our responsibility is to recognize differences (not deficits) and ask ourselves interesting questions about how we can differentiate our instruction as we teach with deep regard for each individual.

Children Living in Poverty

The fact that many children who are poor arrive at the school door should not be a surprise. The United States has the highest relative level of child poverty of all industrialized countries. Further, it ranks 31st among those countries in the gap between the rich and the poor. There are 16,134,000 children in poverty in our nation (21.9%); 7,252,000 are extremely poor (meaning that 9.8% have a family income less than half of the poverty level). Of all these children, 3,248,484 receive cash assistance from Temporary Assistance for Needy Families (TANF) (Children's Defense Fund, 2013). This means that many children are now living in poverty unrelieved by social services. As funding for social services continues to dissolve in our current economy, we can expect this troubling situation to persist or worsen.

Children should not be penalized because they are poor. Assessment at school entry should reflect compassion and concern for the many young children who live in poverty in the United States. Poverty is a form of human suffering; negative ramifications for young children are a sad reality. Why would educators ever compound these ramifications with school-based rejection or disparagement? The mission of the school is to embrace the children who come and to do everything possible to open the doors of opportunity for them (Passow & Elliott, 1968).

WHAT IS READINESS FOR SCHOOL?

Historically, all children were assumed to be ready for school when they reached the designated age of entry. However, as concerns about school accountability, early literacy, and standardized tests have escalated, "readiness" increasingly has been connected to skills, abilities, and characteristics designated as essential for academic success in school (Weigel & Martin, 2006). Although there is a great deal of discussion about readiness for school, there is little or no agreed-upon definition of what it actually is. A broad assumption is that school readiness includes the domains of health, physical development, emotional well-being, social competence, motivation to learn, communication skills, cognition, and general knowledge (Weigel & Martin, 2006).

Actual assessment of readiness varies from school district to school district, and assumptions about the existence of a reliable measure of readiness may be misplaced. Researchers have found that many readiness tests are relatively poor predictors of future school performance and that typical assessment practices lack sufficient reliability and validity for making decisions about school placement (Carlton & Winsler, 1999). For this reason, since 1995, the American Academy of Pediatrics has indicated that screening tests should not be used to keep children of age out of school (Lewit & Baker, 1995).

Considering a lack of consensus on what readiness really is, how it is best evaluated, and how assessments should be used, we logically might wonder why so many negative perceptions of child readiness have permeated school and society. We also might question the value of assessment and related research that persistently targets and labels the abilities and potential of children of color, children who are poor, and children whose first language is not English. This has created bias and low expectations for children without closing the much-discussed achievement gap in the United States.

Social Justice: Aanetra Plans for Readiness

Aanetra knows that many of her current preschool students will be assessed for kindergarten at the end of the school year. She has already overheard some of her colleagues talking about her students; a few have mentioned hoping to get some but not others in their future classrooms. Aanetra has learned a lot in her inclusive classroom; she has a greater recognition of the role she can play in opening up spaces of fairness and equal opportunity for all of her children. The wealthier students seem to be favored by the teachers. She decides to be proactive in preparing her students to be ready for kindergarten and equally proactive in preparing the kindergarten teachers for her students.

The Classroom Plan. Aanetra has read a journal article titled "Getting Ready for School: An Examination of Early Childhood Educato's' Belief Systems" (Lara-Cinisomo, Fuligni, Ritchie, Howes, & Karoly, 2008). She learns that many early childhood teachers tend to perceive children as ready for school when they exhibit confidence, strong communication skills, and the ability to collaborate. Aanetra makes a plan to emphasize those three areas in classroom projects and activities over the next few months.

In thinking about confidence, Aanetra realizes that some of her students are more fearful than others about new people and situations. The children have not always been collaborating very well outside of their circle of friends in the room. She decides to invite several visitors into her classroom to be interviewed by the children. Before each visitor comes, she places the children in small groups carefully designed to include students with special needs and students from every background. During morning center time, she meets with each group to make sure that every child shares an idea for a question he or she might ask the visitor.

As each visitor is interviewed, Aanetra observes child confidence and communication skills carefully. She targets some children, who seem to be having more difficulty, for special encouragement and support as they plan to communicate with the visitor. Aanetra takes photographs of the children with the visitors for her bulletin board, and she also sends the photos home in a newsletter. She asks the families to talk with the children specifically about their group collaboration and the question that they asked the visitor.

The School Plan. Aanetra develops a small booklet focused on each of her students who will be moving to kindergarten next fall. They each have a separate page on which they draw themselves and something they really like to do in school. Aanetra brings the book with her to a series of planning meetings with the kindergarten teachers and emphasizes the strengths of every child. She shows it to her principal as well and urges him to be sure that the children remain integrated in their placements. Her hope is that each kindergarten will have some children with disabilities, some of the children who entered the program through the criteria of financial need, and some of the children who are more affluent. Aanetra wants to do everything she can to be sure that all her students will be treated in a socially just way; she constantly articulates and demonstrates her respect and high regard for every child in her classroom.

CAN READINESS ASSESSMENT BRING HARM TO CHILDREN?

It makes sense, of course, to care about children at the point of school entry and to determine their strengths as well as any needs that should be met as soon as possible. However, it appears that many assessments for readiness measure developmental characteristics more likely to be generated by economic and cultural privilege. Children whose births and early lives have taken place outside of that culture of privilege can be labeled as deficient before they have a fair chance to benefit from what the school has to offer them. We need to ask ourselves whether it is *this presumption of deficiency* that places them more at risk for school failure, particularly when it is reinforced with a belief that there is an inevitable "cumulative deficit" that will place these children in a downward spiral throughout the school years (Dudley-Marling, 2007).

Every year more than 3 million children enroll in a kindergarten program in the United States. Unfortunately, early assessments of these children identify a "school-readiness divide" presumed to be created by socioeconomic factors (Daily, Burkhauser, & Halle, 2011, p. 21). Identified risk factors leading to lower school-entry skills include reception of food stamps or temporary assistance by the family, single parents, mothers with less than a high school education, and a primary language other than English (Maxwell & Clifford, 2004).

These risk factors have remained consistent over time and have long tended to overidentify deficits in children who are poor or who belong to "minorities." The very creation of the Head Start program in 1962 was based on the assumption of deficiencies in children who were poor; the idea of "cultural deprivation" implied a host of negative assumptions about the children as well as their families and communities (Fennimore, 2000). Children of color historically have had the highest rates of kindergarten retention and placement in special education. Further, their families have been most likely to be told to keep them home from school for an extra year because they are immature (Carlton & Winsler, 1999). The children experiencing the greatest challenges outside of school are most likely to encounter barriers when they enter the school door.

CRITIQUING THE "DEFICIT GLAZE"

Children do not profit from entering school with the preconceived perspective that they and their families are deficient and deprived. Such perspectives cover the child with what Dudley-Marling (2007) has termed a "deficit glaze" of pathology that can result in harmful institutional dispositions and practices. When generations of children with certain characteristics are deemed deficient and pathological, the "cumulative gaps" they experience may be largely the result of the ways they are perceived and treated in school (Dudley-Marling, 2007). The children may enter on different levels but they all have potential to learn and grow; it is the schools that can close the doors to some before they have ever truly opened.

Ethics: Jordan Plans for Readiness

Seven of the students in Jordan's rural child-care classroom will be leaving the center to take the bus to an elementary school next fall. It will be a ride of almost an hour each way, and the children will be encountering a completely new environment. Jordan is doing a lot of exciting projects with his mixed-age group, and he feels that the focus on valuing the rural environment has been very productive. However, he does not know the several new teachers in the school that his 5-year-olds will be attending, and he is concerned about how his students will be received.

After reading a journal article titled "Rural Kindergarten Teachers' Perceptions of School Readiness: A Comparison with the Carnegie Study" (Espinosa, Thornburg, & Matthews, 1997) Jordan becomes aware of the tendency of some rural teachers to place higher value on early academic skills in their incoming students. He becomes concerned that his students may not appear to their new teachers to have enough academic skills in math and reading.

The Classroom Plan. Jordan's classroom is rich in experiences in literacy and numeracy. However, because of their mixed ages and the philosophy of the center, there is almost no direct instruction of academic skills. A few of the children are starting to read but overall their skills vary. Jordan consults the NAEYC Code of Ethics for some ideas. He sees that Ideal 1-1.I indicates he should be familiar with the knowledge base of early childhood care and education and stay informed through continuing education and training. Jordan is in graduate school, but none of his courses focus on early literacy or numeracy. Jordan seeks out a professor in the university who specializes in readiness and talks with him about the transition his students will be making.

Based on the suggestions he has received, Jordan creates a new school learning center with a photograph of the school bus as well as the new school. He has weekly boxes of numbers and letters with different independent matching and classification activities. The children may choose this during center time; the activities are differentiated and the children are free to choose their own level of activity. When he has time, Jordan goes over to see what the children are doing and he talks about how the letters and numbers relate to what they will be doing in their new school. He is glad to see that the children have greeted the new center with interest and enthusiasm. He plans to structure it more closely over time on what the children will be doing in their new school.

The School Plan. Jordan looks again at the NAEYC Code of Ethics and thinks about Ideal I-3A.3 suggesting that he support coworkers in meeting their professional needs. He decides to contact the principal at the school his students will attend to ask for a meeting and school tour. His goal is to help his colleagues in the new school to understand and respect his students. Jordan is disappointed when his director says he will have to take a personal day to visit the school; there is no budget for substitutes so teachers can do transitional planning. However, he is happily surprised when he arrives at the school to discover that the two teachers of the combined kindergarten–1st-grade classrooms have been invited to the meeting.

Jordan shows them some of the work the children have been doing in the center and shares some of the projects and activities that have been done in his classroom this year. He talks about the reinforcement of pride in the rural culture. The teachers share ideas about their curriculum and some of the ways in which Jordan can help the children be familiar with their new school and the learning experiences they will encounter.

Jordan plans to inform all his colleagues in the center about his school visit. He also prepares a newsletter for the parents with the photograph of the bus and the school, and tells them about some of the things he is doing to be sure the children have a smooth transition.

RESEARCH AND EARLY CHILDHOOD PROGRAMS

The process of gaining federal, state, or local funding for early childhood programs requires convincing evidence of need. Thus, those who seek funding for such programs for young children often must rely on research establishing delays, lacks, and deficiencies in targeted groups of children. Although these same children undoubtedly have multiple strengths and competencies as well, the latter may be silenced in order to emphasize the need for funding for a program. Once the need has been established, convincing arguments can be made about the ways in which the proposed early childhood program will address deficits to better prepare the children for success in school and society (Fennimore, 2000).

The problem with the above scenario is that a true portrait of the multifaceted child and family is lost. Encased in a deeply negative cast, the worth and social value of those targeted for assistance are demeaned. Michelle Fine (1993) describes this as a process of creating a partial image of a group at risk, setting it apart from the norm, and then creating interventions to "help" that ultimately can increase bias and preserve the inequitable social status quo. The worthy goals of funded programs can be undermined by the damaging images of the children and families that have been further disseminated throughout society.

Critical Analysis of Research

Even when research on children is carefully constructed to be scientific and objective, it does not take place in a cultural vacuum. Pierre Bourdieu (1991) asserted that research always reflects cultural bias in design and hypothesis. It tends to produce theory, language, and practice that favor some aspects of reality while ignoring others. Researchers who use signs and symbols, according to Bourdieu, have linguistic communities that share meaning and assign value to people. The power to value or devalue becomes a form of domination that can easily intimidate those deemed unworthy or inferior (Bourdieu, 1991). When we say that children are superior or inferior, we construct words and images that place them in hierarchies of social status. Such institutional hierarchies can make differential treatment of children seem right and just—even though some children are unfairly privileged while others are marginalized and harmed (MacKinnon, 1992).

Simply stated, some children in the United States enter school with far more cultural capital, such as the resources, experiences, and characteristics that are sought after and valued in society. In their book *Reproduction in Education, Society, and Culture*, Bourdieu and Passeron (1990) identified the ways in which cultural capital becomes a form of sorting and classifying in social institutions. They argued that, within this process, schools actually reproduce the perceived social class in which the children enter. "In America, no less than Europe, credentials contribute to ensuring the reproduction of social inequality" (p. xi). Our challenge as teachers is to refuse to participate in sorting children by social capital, through our constant efforts to look beyond any deficit-based labels and expectations created by early-readiness assessments.

Thinking for Ourselves

Academic freedom is important; it enables scholars and researchers with multiple perspectives to provide the profession and the public with a broad span of publications with insights into important educational problems. However, all educators are responsible for *critical analysis of the information* that is made available to them. It is important to think carefully about inherent issues of power and privilege: Who is being upheld as valued and who is being described as deficient? If we want to stand up for the rights of all children to enter school with a fair chance, we need to make up our own minds about how we choose to receive and process the information we read in scholarly publications.

Analyzing an example. There are many publications that describe the characteristics of children and make predictive statements regarding the connection of their cultural capital to the probability of school success. The example I have chosen for analysis is *Class and Schools: Using Social, Economic, and Educational Reform to Close the Black–White Achievement Gap* (Rothstein, 2004). In this book, the author makes a number of recommendations on how to narrow the achievement gap that focus on school, family, and community resources. In discussing the needs of children who come to school with less cultural capital, he uses the term "lower class," which he defines as:

> a collection of occupational, psychological, personality, health, and economic traits that interact, predicting performance not only in schools but in other institutions as well, that, on average, differs from the performance of families from higher social classes. (p. 4)

Rothstein further indicates:

> As is argued in the book, the influence of social class characteristics *is probably so powerful that schools cannot overcome it, no matter how well trained are their*

teachers and no matter how well designed are their instructional programs and climates. (p. 5, emphasis added)

In a paragraph toward the beginning of his book, Rothstein sets out to "explain how social class differences are likely to affect the academic performance of children" (p. 2). He compares the ways in which the employment conditions of upper middle-class and *lower class parents* have an impact on how they raise their children. Specifically, he analyzes the difference between upper middle-class jobs, in which adults are expected to do such things as collaborate and solve problems, as compared with lower class jobs, which require adults to "follow instructions without question" (p. 2, emphasis added).

Interestingly, Rothstein then interchanges "lower class" and "working class" when indicating, "Children who are raised by parents who are professionals will, on average, have more inquisitive attitudes toward the material presented by their teachers than will children who are raised by *working-class parents*" (p. 2, emphasis added). He concludes the paragraph by indicating that, as a result of employment differences, "no matter how competent the teacher, the academic achievement of lower-class children will, on average, almost inevitably be less" (p. 2). Furthermore, "the probability of this reduced achievement increases as the characteristics of lower-social-class families accumulate" (p. 2).

Respectful reading and critical caution. I believe it is important for educators to carefully consider all perspectives; inevitably, points are made from many different sides of a problem that bear some truth and deserve consideration. However, I selected this example because it provides the opportunity to reflect carefully on the two most important issues I have attempted to raise in this chapter. The first issue is that of denigrating assumptions about some children based only on the cultural capital with which they enter the school, and the second is the presumption that experiences related to a smaller amount of social capital lead to a cumulative deficit beyond the reach of the school.

As educators, we need to acknowledge that there is a great deal of research-based evidence that children with fewer resources tend to do less well in school. However, I would suggest that it is also our responsibility to acknowledge the likelihood that the achievement gap in some ways is created by the attitudes of the school people and the ways in which they label, talk about, and interact with the children who are assumed to be less capable. Further, in light of our ethical responsibility to avoid doing anything harmful to children, I argue that we should maintain an open mind about every child in the context of our own professionalism and sincere desire to see and increase the skills and competencies that every child brings to school.

Respect for Diversity: Emilio Plans for Readiness

Emilio's 3rd-grade students will be transitioning from the bilingual program to a mainly English-only 4th grade next year. He has been preparing them carefully while maintaining a focus on their language heritage. He has read a journal article titled "Effective Strategies for Transitioning Bilingual Students into Mainstream Classrooms" (Peceny, 2011). He is interested in implementing a number of the literacy-based strategies suggested by the article: building more background knowledge before reading texts, team building among the students for literacy understandings, and maintenance of literature logs.

The Classroom Plan. Emilio plans to do more extensive background research on stories the students will be reading in English in their texts. He develops some PowerPoint presentations with photographs that the students will find interesting. After the PowerPoints, the students will work in small groups to relate the information they have been given to their own lives. Emilio will encourage the students to fill out their reading logs in English daily and to note facts and ideas that they have found interesting. As much as possible, he wants to bring the ideas and images in the English texts to life and to help his students make connections with what they read.

The School Plan. Emilio has decided that team building within the school itself is also very important for his students. He wants to build leadership skills that will help them establish their identities within the school. He decides to develop a service project for his class. The local library is in danger of losing funds; people in the community have been asked to write letters to local politicians. *"Todos en la comunidad necesitan la biblioteca. Trabajemos juntos para tratar de mantenerla abierta. Necesitamos escribirle cartas a los funcionarios electos de nuestra comunidad para explicarles porque nuestra biblioteca es muy importante para nosotros."* ["Everyone in the community needs the library. Let's work together to try to keep it open. We need to write letters to those who are elected to help our community to explain why our library is so important to us all."]

Emilio has asked several teachers with whom he is friendly whether his students might come to speak briefly about the project in their classrooms; the students have already written their own letters and will be providing contact information for local politicians to the other children. His students have made a poster display about the library budget cuts and will use it to give a brief presentation at a school assembly.

What is your own cultural experience? I assume that many readers of this book share in my experience of knowing, being related to, and loving people who might be considered "lower class" or "working class." I, for example, am thinking of my beautiful grandmother for whom I was named. A teenaged immigrant from Czechoslovakia, Beatrice Vydra married my Czechoslovakian immigrant grandfather Joseph Schneller and gave birth to five children, including my father, on the East Side of New York City. In 1918, my grandfather was one of the millions of people worldwide who died suddenly in the Spanish influenza epidemic, leaving my shocked grandmother to support and raise her very young children, aged 3 months to 9 years old, alone. Her incredible courage, intelligence, and hard work enabled her to make a modest income with a small business while raising her children with devotion and love. All five of her children, who experienced poverty, lived remarkable and productive lives. (My father insisted that he and his pals had more fun playing ball with broomsticks on the streets of New York in the early 1900s than any child ever had subsequently with expensive, customized toys.)

As I write, I am thinking also of many different people for whom I have great admiration. We have a public service employee in our community, for example, who falls somewhere in the "lower class" and "working class" definition. She is an amazing and devoted mother and grandmother who goes between her first and second minimum-wage jobs 7 days a week. Always deeply concerned with the academic progress of her grandchildren, this loving woman is a leader not only in her family, but in our community. She recently was honored at an organizational dinner for all the contributions she has made as an outstanding public servant.

Another person I raise for consideration, one of many I might mention, is a former African American student who was enrolled a number of years ago in one of my graduate classes in New York City. During a class discussion of a book on poverty, a student in the class asserted that the major problem with poverty was the fact that poor parents in public housing projects did not care about education. My African American student proudly rose to her feet and expressed tearful emotions about such assumptions. She said, "I have listened to people talk about my mother like this since I began my doctoral studies! I'm constantly reading it in books and articles! This makes me furious! I grew up in this city in what you are calling 'public housing projects' and what *my family* called *our neighborhood.* My wonderful single mother was completely devoted to our academic success!"

When my oldest daughter received her graduate degree from the University of Pennsylvania, former president Jimmy Carter gave the graduation speech. At one point, while urging social responsibility, he asked the families of the graduates to consider the ways in which they treated their maids. The young woman seated next to my daughter in the assembled group of graduates turned to her and said, "What's he talking about? My mother *was* a maid!"

The danger of generalizations. The point that I want to make with these brief stories is that a critical analysis of what we read should lead us to a number of important *questions*. What is the cultural and socioeconomic background of authors, and how has it influenced their perspectives? What issues of power and privilege are reflected in the writing? Is there a "dysconsciousness" that sees the inequitable status quo as *inevitable* and beyond the reach of the school? If so, who stands to benefit? How might this book or article be received by those who are described in deficit-based terms? How might they articulate their strengths and their hope for their children? Would they be shocked to learn that their trust in the schools is misplaced—that some educators look down on their children and assume that they will never do as well as affluent children whose families hold professional jobs?

Focusing on what can be done. Generalizations are partial views at best—they leave out all the individual differences that have an impact on the lives of children at every level of society. I would argue that our work as educators must stay focused on what can be done for our students; nothing is to be gained with denigrating generalizations or negative predictions. There is no question that family income and education level have an impact on children, or that desperate life circumstances can get in the way of academic attainment. But as educators, our best work can be done only if we commit ourselves to providing an outstanding education to the children who enter the doors of our schools and classrooms.

THE OTHER ALTERNATIVE: THE "READY SCHOOL"

When children are tested to see whether they meet the entry standards of school, the burden of proof is placed on them and their families. The school gets to define readiness and then locate any problems in meeting its construction of readiness standards within the child (Carlton & Winsler, 1999). The alternative stance is that schools should assume, except in the case of extreme circumstances, that every child entering school is ready to learn (Lewit & Baker, 1995). Further, the school should evaluate *itself* for readiness to meet the needs of incoming children from the stance of the physical, emotional, social, and cognitive needs of the child.

Readiness for school is not the same thing as readiness to learn. Children may come to school from a variety of cultural backgrounds, some of which are far more closely aligned than others to the specific culture of the institution. Thus, it may take longer or require greater effort on the part of the school before all children have adjusted to the particular learning environment. *All* of the children, however, are ready to *learn*, and that learning quickly may increase their readiness for school.

Readiness is neither static nor located in biological or cultural capital; Vygotsky indicated that learning and experience often *precede and lead* developmental growth (Carlton & Winsler, 1999). The flexible school environment is capable of adjusting expectations while keeping them high; all children can attain goals, but some need more time or differential approaches to learning. Most important is the creation of a warm and supportive environment that is conducive to learning, one that honors children and respects their interests, culture, language, and family life.

Advocacy: Kira Plans for Readiness

Kira has been concerned all year about perceived bias toward her students in the transitional kindergarten. Her initial hesitance to be more proactive with other teachers has begun to change; she did speak with both the library teacher and her principal about the punitive way in which her students had been treated in a former library period. Although she maintained a professional demeanor and chose her words carefully, her advocacy for her students was very much in evidence. Kira is now determined to work with her students toward a positive experience in 1st grade next year.

The Classroom Plan. Kira read an article titled "Kindergarten Teachers' Reported Use of Kindergarten to First Grade Transition Practices" (La Paro & Pianta, 2000). This article made her aware of the expectation of many 1st-grade teachers that children will take more responsibility for autonomy in meeting school expectations. Kira decides to focus on helping the children in her room to be more independent in following directions and completing activities and assignments. She gives a specific amount of time for some work to be completed and teaches them how to look at the clock as they work so they can finish on time. Kira also encourages the children to listen to directions carefully, ask questions right away, and then try to finish assignments on their own. The children are doing well with her increased expectations.

The School Plan. Kira decides to get to school earlier in the morning and start dropping by the classrooms of the 1st-grade teachers to say hello. She makes it a point to chat in a friendly way about how well her students are doing in developing more autonomy. She also is going to try to arrange for her students to visit all the 1st-grade classes in the coming month and to sit with the children for their morning meeting. Kira has placed the words WE ARE READY on the door of her classroom, underneath which she has a list of 50 words that mean "success."

Kira also has decided to write a "Hippocratic Oath" for teachers that she will display in her classroom. This is what it says:

> *As a teacher, I consider every child to be a worthy person and a capable learner. My goal is to have all my students leave my classroom with a better sense of who they are and what they are capable of doing and becoming. My language as a professional will not include negative labels or words that disparage children, families, or communities. I will focus persistently on the strengths of my students and use those strengths to help them overcome any challenges or barriers they face as learners. My goal is to lead my students and my colleagues by example by modeling positive attitudes, hard work, dedication to the common good, and unflagging hope for the future of all my students.*

DEMOCRATIC APPROACHES TO READINESS

While writing this chapter, I consulted the yellow-paged publication *Infant and Child in the Culture of Today*, written in 1943 by famed maturationists Arnold Gesell and Frances Ilg. In the preface, Gesell wrote, "This book is written and completed in the midst of a war which is bringing untold misery to countless infants and children. And the aftermath has not yet come" (p. ix). This served as a reminder to me that every generation must address the needs of children in the context of serious social dilemmas, whether they are war, disaster, poverty, or other forms of unrest and inequality. *Compassion* is absolutely essential to every generation of educators as we reach out to inform and prepare children for productive lives.

Gesell emphasized "considerateness" (p. 10) as a democratic way to regard developing children. The very word, as he saw it, conveyed deep respect for the individual. His thoughts are far from outdated; they have a great deal to offer educators today as they consider the topic of readiness. Inasmuch as we have advanced as a technological society since World War II, we may well have lost considerable ground in civility and humane treatment of young children. This is a very good time in history to revisit the idea of readiness in the context of democracy—and to reconstruct warm and caring early school environments in which children who are respected as unique individuals can flourish.

SOME PRACTICAL IDEAS FOR GETTING STARTED

It is very likely that conceptualizations of "readiness" have permeated your thinking about young children. These may have come from classes you have taken or books you have read; your own program or school may have readiness policies and assessments. This chapter has suggested that you turn from a focus on readiness in the child to the readiness of the school—and thus in yourself as a teacher.

Reflect on Your Beliefs and the Language You Use

Popular conceptualizations of readiness have changed the ways in which some educators speak about children. An enthusiastic statement such as, "I cannot wait to meet my new students," might become, "I have so many students coming who can't recognize all the letters of the alphabet." Make a conscious effort to shift to a language of *inquiry*—"I am looking forward to trying a number of new strategies that will help my incoming children become familiar with the alphabet," or, "I am excited to see the ways in which the new books in my classroom help the children to get interested in reading." Make a habit of turning judgment into enthusiasm—be a teacher who loves a challenge and looks forward to meeting the needs of all students.

Make Increased Readiness One of Your Goals as a Teacher

Our hypothetical teacher-guides demonstrated both a classroom- and school-based approach to readiness in children. Each teacher read an informative journal article and implemented some of the ideas in that article to prepare students for upcoming school transitions. Further, each teacher made a decision about a way to have an impact on the school and the future relationships of his or her students with other teachers.

In your own setting, think about how readiness is discussed and how it shapes the actions of teachers. Then, plan for ways in which you can help the children in your care to be ready for transitions even as you try to open minds and doors to them in the school setting. Our teacher-guides provide some ideas of how to do this from the standpoint of social justice, ethics, respect for diversity, and advocacy.

Questions for Discussion

1. What is the conceptualization of readiness in your school or program, and how does it affect the school-entry experiences of the children?

2.   What do you recall about your own entry into school? Were you tested or assessed? Are you aware of any impact this may have had on the way you were perceived by your teachers?

3.   Are you in the habit of thinking critically about what you are reading concerning the relationship of cultural capital to child success in school? Have professors or books you have read created an assumption that children who are poor inevitably will do less well in school?

4.   In what ways can you use educational research about school readiness to support readiness-based skills and abilities in your students?

5.   How might you help other teachers in your school or program to appreciate the abilities and overall competency of the children you teach?

Six

Democratic Classrooms
Visible Commitments in the Everyday

We turn our attention in this chapter to the many ways in which our strongest commitments as teachers can become a visible and dynamic force in our classrooms. Young children are ready to begin initial explorations of ethics, social justice, respect for diversity—and even advocacy! Teaching these concepts, however, is never as simple as the implementation of good ideas for activities or thematic units. The true foundation of the democratic classroom is dynamic social interchange facilitated by teachers with a vision of social change. The curriculum plays an important role, of course, and there are many excellent sources for lesson and unit ideas. Ultimately, however, everything that we teach in our classroom is shaped by our values, beliefs, commitments, and determination to awaken our students to the possibilities of democracy.

It is important to acknowledge at the outset that every day is a *busy day* in the classroom! Teachers are continually called upon to balance their carefully planned curriculum with the unexpected events that inevitably arise. Young children are demanding and often unpredictable; parents, colleagues, and administrators unexpectedly may require our attention and assistance as well. It is a given that teaching young children requires flexibility, energy, and resilience.

It is because our daily lives as teachers are so demanding that our good intentions must become *firm habits of mind*. Even in the midst of what might feel at times like chaos, our well-established commitment to be just and ethical teachers can continually emerge to guide our thoughts and actions. We do have the power and ability to construct positive classroom communities in which our students learn how to be not only successful learners but good citizens as well.

THE DEMOCRATIC CLASSROOM COMMUNITY

A democratic classroom is one in which young children learn how to balance the rights and responsibilities of citizenship. They are expected to enjoy their own opportunities and rights in a context of awareness of the needs and equal rights of others. It is *social communication* that helps children to explore the pathways of citizenship in shared spaces; thus the democratic classroom is one in which positive relationships are encouraged and a collaborative exchange of ideas is valued.

As a teacher, it is important for you to provide physical, emotional, and cognitive spaces for relationships between children to be formed. Your students need to interact with one another as they engage in all of the negotiations that arise in the classroom—decisionmaking, sharing, helping others, and resolving conflict. Many of the most important lessons of democratic living come not from our planned curriculum but from the ways in which children interrelate and the methods through which their teachers help them to process information and resolve conflicts and difficulties throughout the day (Schniedewind & Davidson, 1998).

TALKING ABOUT DIFFERENCES IN THE CLASSROOM

Language is the essential vehicle of democracy; it provides open avenues for the negotiation of interest in self and regard for the others. Your classroom should be characterized by a lively exchange of conversation in which all voices are heard and valued. You, as the teacher, set the tone by conversing with your students about many topics and inviting different ideas and points of view.

If you teach children in the upper ranges of early childhood, you may well have a structured academic curriculum. This does not need to preclude a wide variety of classroom conversations. Take advantage of opportunities to stress the idea of community; have group meetings with the students to discuss social problems that emerge. Do everything you can to encourage shared conversations throughout the day and plan subject-based lessons to encourage discussion among students. Be aware of conflict or unkindness among students, and provide the structure for resolution that includes respectful concern for everyone involved.

Children benefit from classroom environments in which honest talk about all kinds of human differences is encouraged and supported. This kind of climate is modeled in *Starting Small* (Teaching Tolerance Project, 1997)—a book (and film) focused on the anti-bias strategies of selected early childhood programs for young children. One teacher has these words displayed in her room: "Let's talk. Let's all talk. What we don't talk about hurts us all" (p. 2). She invites genuine conversation about real people and real events that take place in and outside of the classroom.

Young children need to be able to wonder openly about differences between people—shades of skin color, kinds of bodies, ways of speaking, and assistive devices for children with disabilities. Nothing should be taboo or "not nice" to discuss; differences should be *named* and appreciated as students and teachers do the intellectual and emotional work of recognizing what can unite people or keep them apart (Schniedewind & Davidson, 1998). Acknowledging what can divide and separate is an important component in establishing pathways to acceptance and inclusion in your classroom.

Jordan Opens Spaces for Talk

Jordan has continued his curriculum focus on the positive aspects of life in a rural community as well as on his new efforts to prepare the children who will be taking the bus to the consolidated school district next year. However, during his recent visit to their new school, he noticed a number of children who appeared to be immigrants from other nations as well as children who were Hispanic or African American. Because of some new construction and industry in the area of the elementary school, it was likely that more people representing many kinds of diversity would continue to move to the area.

When Jordan gave this more thought, he realized that his students had little experience in talking with one another about many of the differences they might soon encounter. They were accustomed to the arrival of some children of migrant workers at different times of the year, and knew that many of them spoke Spanish. However, other than that, there was definitely room to expand their experience and thinking about diversities such as skin color, clothing, and a variety of languages in the center. Jordan decided that this was a good time to get his students talking about human differences.

Jordan created a display on an interactive bulletin board that said: WHO IS THIS? WHAT DO YOU WANT TO KNOW? He had copied a number of photographs of children from around the world from the Internet and planned to place a different one on the bulletin board every few days. At first, however, he put a group picture of all the children in his class on the board. He encouraged the children to ask one another about what they liked to eat or what kind of games they liked to play.

Then, he began to put up pictures of children wearing clothing that would be unfamiliar to his students and encouraged them to think of what questions they would like to ask. At first the children were quiet; then they began to ask, "Why are you wearing that funny dress?" or, "What is that thing on your head?" Jordan responded to all of the questions with information only; he wanted the children to feel natural about asking questions. During subsequent morning meetings he started to discuss ways of asking people about themselves in a kind and welcoming way.

Jordan then began to display pictures of children with darker skin color and in different kinds of international settings. He was aware of some negative sentiments toward both groups in the community and listened carefully to the children's questions and conversation. He heard some comments from the children that concerned him, but again decided not to interfere at that time. He continued to bring up topics of diversity at the morning meeting, talking about the bulletin board and encouraging discussion about human differences. He was very clear in articulating his own commitments: "I respect all people and believe that all people are equal to one another. It is interesting to me when people look different; I want to be their friend and find out all about them!"

Finally, Jordan put all the pictures together on the bulletin board and referred to them frequently throughout the day. As the children were more accustomed to looking at and talking about the pictures, he entered their discussion and helped them to process their thinking about differences. Jordan felt that the children were more sensitive in framing questions and indicating a deeper acceptance of and interest in differences.

DESIGNING THE SOCIAL ENVIRONMENT

It is interesting to think about designing classrooms with an eye toward the development of democratic and caring relationships between children. There should be spaces in which children can relax, meet, and talk with one another. Tables and chairs can be strategically placed to promote conversation and sharing. It is also helpful to have a space where the teacher and children can talk together, share information, and negotiate problems and difficulties that emerge during the school day. Pictures of children talking with adults and other children might be placed strategically around the room to encourage conversation as a social norm. Teachers constantly should seek to demonstrate their respect for friendly conversation among children and adults.

Everyone Belongs

You, as the teacher, set the tone for respect for diversity in your classroom. The children in your room should know from their very first day in school that you intend to create a fair and welcoming classroom community. To "belong" in a democratic classroom is to have the opportunity to develop a positive self-identity in the context of respect for the identities of others. Your classroom should contain photographs, drawings, and cultural artifacts that reflect the lives of all the children in the room (e.g., housing, clothing, and neighborhoods). It is also important to select books and other materials that reflect the languages (words from every language spoken should be displayed) and differences (e.g., photographs should reflect various shades of skin color and different family formations) that children bring with them to school. Pictures of differences that are not in your actual classroom should be included as well. Don't forget that you as the teacher are by far the most important resource in the room! It is you who will engage in the constant positive interactions that help children to negotiate the balance between knowledge of self and awareness of others.

Aanetra Refreshes Her Focus on "Everyone Belongs"

Aanetra is proud of the many efforts this year to promote inclusion and a sense of cohesion among all the children and families who are a part of the pre-K program. Her efforts to help her students increase their readiness for kindergarten, through group activities and interviewing visitors, were successful. She did notice, however, that some children were very confident with the visitors while others remained shy and reticent. The children who were more confident belonged to a group that knew one another from their community and had tended to consistently seek one another out for play.

Aanetra respects the individual differences and preferences of her students, but also wants to make sure that she has done everything possible to support their social development. She reflects on the fact that all of her students will move to a kindergarten next year or the year after, and decides that a return the next month to her initial focus on "a community is where everyone belongs" may be very helpful to all of them. She starts by reading the children a book about a child who is new to a classroom, and helps them think back to what it felt like to be new in her classroom last fall. "I want to be sure," she says, "that each and every one of you knows that you belong to this classroom and to one another—you are a group of friends in our classroom community." Then, she goes on to explain that their lives will be full of new classrooms in which everyone will belong, and that she wants them all to know how to be leaders in being friends and making friends in any new setting.

Aanetra takes a new group picture of her class and prints out an enlargement to place in the class meeting center. During morning meeting for the next few days, she engages the children in a discussion of what each of them can do to make the classroom a place in which everyone feels very welcome. She emphasizes the responsibility they have to be aware of one another's feelings and remember to say and do welcoming things every day. The children come up with some ideas on their own about ways to welcome and help people:

"It is nice to see you this morning."
"I like the color of your shirt."
"Can I help you carry that?"
"Let's sit together at lunch."

For the next few weeks, she is going to assign each child to a different partner every day and encourage all the children to be sure that they help their partners feel welcome in the classroom community. She makes a partner chart and talks with the children about what they have done or plan to do to be a kind friend. As a culminating activity, Aanetra invites another class to join hers for a short movie and snack. Before they come, she plans with her class to make sure that every child will be a greeter and friend to one of the visitors. "Children," she says, "all your life I want you to be the kind of person who always helps other people to feel welcome with others in a group."

Aanetra also begins to take anecdotal notes on children during play and work times. In addition to spontaneous notes, she focuses on five children a week. By doing this, she hopes to individualize the forms of encouragement that she gives to each child. Some may need more of a sense of belonging and more assertiveness in joining groups, while others may need to become more skilled in inclusive talk and behaviors.

Teachers learn from questions. When we welcome all kinds of questions from children, we can learn a great deal about what they actually are thinking. This information is invaluable for future planning. For example, I remember bringing a group of 4- and 5-year-olds to the performance of a small theater troupe designed to help young children understand different disabilities. The adult actors portrayed children who were disabled in various ways; they were very believable and the children thought that they actually were disabled. When the actors invited questions, one of my students raised her hand right away and asked them all, "How did you get that way?"

This opened my eyes to the importance of explaining the genesis of disability to my students. While I often had stressed inclusion and acceptance, I had overlooked the possibility that my students might have been curious about the ways in which disabilities actually came into being. When we returned to the classroom to talk about the performance that we had seen, I explained that many children with disabilities had been born with them. Their parents had welcomed them with love, and the doctors and nurses had helped the parents to understand and take care of their babies just as they help all new parents.

Disabilities were only part of a person, I explained, so it was important to get to know everything about the people. I also told them that people can become disabled later in life because of accidents or illness; we need to get to know everything about those people too. I continued to stress inclusion and acceptance in my teaching, but also focused more on the ways in which human differences come about. When children have the opportunity to ask questions, they will lead their teachers in designing curriculum for depth of learning and understanding.

DEMOCRATIC CLASSROOMS ARE MORAL CLASSROOMS

Shared life in democratic classrooms supports the moral development that is the foundation for ethical thought. To this end, you as the teacher can find many ways to support the growing interest of your students in *rightness* of treating people in kind and considerate ways. Children *become moral* by grappling with social issues that are a natural part of their lives. Such issues include aggression, fair use of materials, and equal opportunity to participate in desired classroom opportunities. It is important to note that the morality of children is not interchangeable with *adult-imposed* obedience, sharing, or politeness. Moral children are *thinking* children who use their *own cognitive skills* to deliberate carefully on their obligation to others (DeVries & Zan, 1994).

Robert Coles, in his book *The Moral Intelligence of Children* (1997), shared a story he frequently used to engage children in conversations about morality. In the story, titled "Starry Time," a little girl named Stella has a bedroom full of beautiful stars all her own. She assumes that all children have stars in their bedrooms but discovers through conversation with classmates that her situation is actually unique. Even the moon in the dark night sky tells her sadly of his deep loneliness.

After Stella deliberates thoughtfully on her situation, she decides to tell her stars that it is not right for her to keep them all to herself. One night, she urges them to fly up to the sky to join the moon, so that people everywhere can enjoy their bright lights. The stars race excitedly around her bedroom in a circular farewell embrace, and then fly out the window up into the waiting sky. The next day when Stella leaves her house she overhears many excited conversations between her friends in school about new stars twinkling last night in the once dark evening sky. Stella has changed the world.

The Power of Moral Stories

I have read the story of Stella to many groups of children and teachers, and it has never failed to inspire. Stella is quite remarkable; she realizes that she has sole possession of something incredibly beautiful, and responds with a growing awareness of her social responsibility. The more she sees how the absence of the light of the stars is affecting others, the more she is convinced that sharing them is the right thing to do. Ultimately, the entire world is brightened by her generosity. Stella has not lost her stars—she can see them gleaming nightly—but she has found her best self in the context of generous concern for others.

By using stories like this in our classrooms, we can help our students to avoid being swept into "the moral undertow"—a life that responds only to one's personal wishes and transient moods without regard for human rights and ethical obligations to others (Coles, 1997). What could Stella's stars represent to the children in your class? You might explain them as her talents and gifts—the unique things that she could contribute to the world. Then, you could help your children imagine something very special that they also might contribute to the world. Even very young children can think about the special things that only they can accomplish!

It would be a good idea for them to also think about their contribution to the classroom they now share. This might lead to an art project, possibly a mural, on which each child contributes a representation of an act of helping in the classroom. All the traditional "class helper" tasks might now take on a more substantial meaning—doing your fair share is the *right* thing to do when you live in a community and it has a significant impact on the lives of others.

Teachers Model Social Behaviors

It is of critical importance for children to see the adults in their lives model moral actions and behaviors. Children are confused by a lack of coherence between what they are told to do and the behaviors they observe in adults. As they mature, this lack of coherence can cause a demoralizing sense of hypocrisy. For example, an elementary school-aged boy featured in Coles's (1997) book on moral intelligence responds to a discussion of morality and hypocrisy with these words: "My dad says a lot of people talk a good line . . . but their scorecard isn't so good, because talk is cheap" (p. 17).

Of course, we teachers want a very good "scorecard"! This is why the line of integrity between what we say and what we do is essential. To a great degree, children develop moral intelligence through observation of the ways in which other people act. While it is true that their families play a central role in this learning, we teachers should not lose sight of the fact that we are also important role models. "The child is a witness; the child is an ever-attentive witness of grown-up morality . . . or lack thereof. The child looks and looks for cues as to how one ought to behave" (Coles, 1997, p. 5).

Our own daily habits of mind should include mindfulness of virtues such as kindness, compassion, respect, truthfulness, and trustworthiness. These virtues may be tested by many challenging events and interactions in our schools and classrooms. Through their demonstration, however, we display competence in all the admirable qualities that we hope to inspire in our students. Teachers and children together have the interactive power to develop an environment of moral and ethical development on a daily basis.

CLASSROOM RULES: IMPORTANT LESSONS IN DEMOCRACY

As indicated above, children develop morality through opportunities to respond thoughtfully to situations in their daily lives. Many if not most classrooms have rules—often posted in visible places. They tend to be one of the first things that I notice when I enter a classroom. While rules do not in and of themselves create morality in children, they can help children to develop critical insights into the relationship of laws to life in society. Rules are essential to the maintenance of reasonable order in classrooms and schools; they represent forms of authority that are essential to civic learning.

That being said, the subject of children and classroom rules is very complex. Rules should keep children safe and provide them with a moral, social, and cognitive structure for development. In addition, rules should provide a rich context in which children can learn about power and authority. There should be a connection between the rules in their classroom and the laws they will be expected to follow as adults. Rules (like laws) should exist to delineate responsibility and protect the rights of all citizens. However, the way in which rules are described and presented to children is of great importance. This requires careful thought on the part of teachers—how should rules be phrased and displayed in classrooms?

When I discuss classroom rules with my undergraduate students or with teachers in professional development, I often start with a discussion of the rule that I have seen most often in the many classrooms I have visited over the years: "Keep your hands and feet to yourself."

I ask those in attendance to imagine attending a social occasion such as a concert or a wedding and discovering the words "keep your hands and feet to yourself" in the event program. How might they respond? Laughter is almost always the first response. Further discussion, however, reveals that such language would be considered by many to be offensive and inappropriate. Then I ask why, if we would find these words to be brash and lacking in social grace, they are so often displayed on the lists of rules in classrooms filled with children.

Our class rules should be in place to teach more than self-control. Rules, after all, exist to create order and to protect the equal rights of everyone who shares life in a community. In the case of the goals behind "keep your hands and feet to yourself," I think we want to *teach* children two things. The first is that they have the right to adequate personal working space for their bodies and belongings in the classroom. The second is that this right comes with a democratic responsibility to respect the personal working space that also belongs to everyone else.

Classroom rules should be worded in ways that model respect for children. How, for example, might we change, "Keep your hands and feet to yourself," to a rule that respects children as it teaches an important democratic concept? I would suggest, "Each person in our classroom must respect the right of all others to their own space and materials." Is this too long and complex for young children? Possibly, but I think it would provide an interesting opportunity for a democratic discussion of the reasoning behind the rule. When many people share one space, the space needs to be well organized so everyone will be comfortable and empowered to do their work. If everyone can enjoy their own space while respecting the space of others, then *everyone's* rights and needs are respected. It is very important for children to see the ways in which rules *help and protect them* as well as others.

CHILDREN'S RULES AND CHILDREN'S RIGHTS

A university professor enters an elementary school to visit a student teacher. It is "just say no to drugs day" in this school, and the professor walks under a huge, colorful banner that says "JUST SAY NO" hanging over the entry of the school. Proceeding to the school playground, the professor finds her student teacher seated next to a weeping young child on the "punishment bench." This child, like all the children on the playground, is wearing a button that says, "Just say no." When the professor asks why the child is being punished, the student teacher says, "A teacher asked him to do something, and he said no."

This is an actual event I experienced years ago while supervising student teachers. It troubled me then, and it still embodies the problem of the mixed-up messages that young children can receive in school. In this case, I believed it was possible that this young child thought "just say no day" meant he could say "no." I wondered if anyone had taken the time that day to explain the difference between the abstract concept of resisting illegal drug use later on in life and "just saying no" that day? Or was that sign put up in the hallway and the buttons placed on the clothing of the children without an adequate explanation of how "just say no" should be interpreted?

The small boy crying on the bench may have left school upset and certain of only one thing—when teachers say "just say no" they don't mean it! Such confusion is unnecessary and interferes with children's developing sense of democratic rights and responsibilities. Children need rational explanations of school events, and their teachers should be sensitive to possible confusion. We teachers should know what we consider to be the "rights" of children and protect those rights in the school.

Thinking About Children's Rights

Children's rights have long been a subject of global attention. The United Nations Convention on the Rights of the Child (UNCRC) of 1989 was the first irreducible and legally binding international instrument to provide a full range of human rights to children (UNICEF, 2013). Advocates have not been successful in urging the United States to ratify the convention; it is one of two nations worldwide that have not done so (Somalia is the other) (Hall & Rudkin, 2011). Nonetheless, it is important for all educators to know about and reflect on changing conceptualizations of children's rights adopted by most of the nations of the world.

Traditional approaches to children's rights in the United States have focused on child protection by adults. The UNCRC, while also focused on adult protection, has moved further toward providing children with freedom of thought and expression. They have a right to engage in the processes that have an impact on them, and their perspective should be a part of decisionmaking on their behalf. Further, they should be informed of their rights and be empowered to speak for themselves (Hall & Rudkin, 2011). The reality of how these rights can and should play out in school and society is still in development. However, the UNCRC definitely moves our global society from thinking about children as under adult control to conceptualizing them as capable of making decisions that determine their own destiny to a much greater extent than they do now.

Rights and Authentic Participation

Although our nation has not endorsed the UNCRC, many teachers do provide children with opportunities that could be considered rights-related. For example, young children often are assumed to have the right of *choice* in terms of play centers or books to read. Or, they might be included as rightful partners with their teachers in discussing and shaping classroom decisions that are important to them. As we consider such opportunities for children, I think it is important to consider the presence of *authenticity*. Children cannot learn the lessons of democracy when they are told that they have rights that in fact do not exist. When we educators give "rights" to children, it is important to analyze those rights carefully to avoid coercion and construct a sense of logic and integrity.

For example, we might tell children that they each have the right to choose a learning center . . . *but* that only five children are allowed to play in a center at a time. Thus their right is limited by a teacher-made rule as well as a responsibility to consider the rights of the five children who get there first. In fact, they may end up unable to exercise their "right" to make the choice. How and why some children get there before others is an important consideration, as is how teachers make sure that every child who expressed an interest in a center ultimately has the opportunity to engage in it.

Likewise, if we indicate that the children have the right to participate in a decision (choice of a class trip, for example), we also need to stress their democratic responsibility to accept the majority opinion. And, if some children dissented from the ultimate choice, it is important to name and honor their dissent and refrain from future statements such as, "this is the trip we all decided to make." I think it is a good idea to let children know that adults also have opportunities to have an equal voice in decisions that don't always go the way they would like them to. They will benefit from knowing that we all need to accept the decision of the majority and open our minds to the appreciation of the option that was not our first choice.

Authenticity and Participation in Class Rules

Many of the teachers and students with whom I work have been exposed to the idea that children should participate in creating the rules of the classroom. It often is suggested that the participation of the children supports "buy-in"—they may be more likely to accept the rules because they have had a fair chance to discuss them. It certainly seems logical to include children in a discussion of rules that helps them to feel more personally connected to the behavioral expectations in the classroom.

However, I have some questions about the authenticity of this form of inclusion in classroom governance. We mean well, of course, and the children are often eager to discuss rules. However, most often the rules will not be finalized and governed by children. Rather, they will be under the control of the teacher, who has the power to implement them, identify transgressors, and assign consequences. Ultimately, the rules are not negotiable—they are in fact laws regulated by adults. Children who argue later about the rules may be viewed as defiant, although their opinion was solicited previously. This is why I believe that careful thought is necessary before children are involved in the formulation of rules for the classroom.

Rules and laws. First of all, I believe that children need to understand the difference between laws that are made and governed by those in authority and rules that are community-made in true negotiation. Thus, I think teachers should give full disclosure to the fact that some school rules are really "laws"; they are non-negotiable and created by adults who are in charge. These laws are related to the responsibility of keeping children safe and maintaining order in buildings that contain many people (e.g., remaining completely silent during a fire drill or staying in the classroom with your teacher until the monitor comes to escort you safely to the bus). Children need to know that such rules must not be broken, for good reasons. They also need to understand that laws exist in the larger society, and that it is in everyone's best interest to obey them.

Laws are a complicated topic! While supporting the importance of laws, teachers in some circumstances find that they need to be sensitive to the children whose experiences with legal authorities have been troubling or confusing. Those children may have been witnesses to violent interactions between police and citizens in their communities, or have family members who are currently in prison. Possibly they may have been removed from their family home under parent protest for their own protection. Children might have undocumented family members who are very fearful of being discovered by police or other legal authorities. When these realities exist in children's lives, teachers will be called upon to acknowledge them. If children raise these topics during class discussions, it will be important to listen respectfully and try to help them process their experiences in the context of discussions of rules and democracy.

Are all laws good laws? Children should be helped to see the role of laws in social order; in many ways, they help people to share public spaces and get along with one another. However, our increasingly media-savvy child population may know from television and other sources that some laws (such as current proposed voting restrictions) are contested. In addition, we or other teachers may read children books about human rights movements in which people used civil disobedience to fight wrongful laws.

Thus, on one hand, I think we need to use caution in stressing unquestioning obedience to all laws. But on the other hand, we do want children to know that laws (such as laws against speeding on highways, crossing streets against red traffic lights, or stealing what belongs to others) exist to protect people's rights and keep them safe. I think the most important focus for young children is an understanding that groups of people can work together to solve problems and create rules that help people to get along together. To this end, teachers might create learning experiences that encourage children to discuss *their own ideas about social rules* and the ways in which *they should all treat one another* in the classroom.

Children's Rules for Social Relationships in the Classroom

Young children are capable of posing and discussing rules that might govern their relationships in the classroom. This kind of activity supports their moral development and also gives them an authentic voice in their classroom community (DeVries & Zan, 1994). Teachers can gently mediate such discussions and encourage the children to focus on the importance of nurturing their relationships with one another. The ultimate goal should be an opportunity for them to think about creating a balance between individual needs and the common good (Hall & Rudkin, 2011). Younger children may suggest rules such as:

"No one should say unkind things to anyone."
"We should help our friends when they are crying."
"No pushing when we play kickball in the yard."
"Everyone should help during clean-up times."

Teachers can further help children to think about how they will know whether the rules are successful (e.g., everyone plays kickball and no one is pushed) or they are not (e.g., there is still pushing and we need to think of a better rule). Through this kind of rule-making activity, children can develop the skills of negotiation and a sense of confidence in their ability to solve group problems. They will have an authentic opportunity to pose rules, navigate their implementation, and evaluate their helpfulness in the class community.

As children discuss and construct social rules, they also can pose possible resolutions to conflict. They often need help in developing the words that should be used when another child is creating a conflict in the classroom. It is also useful for children to talk about when they should try to solve a problem on their own and when they should ask an adult for help.

Teachers, while always responsible for child safety, should not rush in to solve classroom conflicts too quickly. In the absence of violence or escalating crisis, children are often capable of solving problems on their own (Hall & Rudkin, 2011). Careful teacher observation will lead to a better understanding of the problem-solving skills the children have, as well as those that continue to be developed and supported in the classroom (Levin, 2003). Such observation can help teachers to plan future learning activities.

Emilio Helps Students Address Conflicts

Emilio has seen some positive changes in his students since they have had more contact with other children in the school; they all seemed to enjoy the public service project. A thank-you letter from the library has been placed in a central location in the classroom, and it is a considerable source of pride for everyone. However, Emilio has sensed some tension in the school hallways between his students and those in other classes, and he also has overheard his students speaking in Spanish about problems with other children in the school. He decides to have a class meeting to talk about what is going on.

As it turns out, the visits that his students have made to other classrooms have created a few problems. Some of the children in other classrooms made fun of his students and pretended to speak Spanish. Two girls overheard someone say, "Those are the kids who can't speak English." Apparently, a few children stuck their feet out in the aisles when his students left the stage during the assembly. The interpretation of his students was that those children were trying to trip them. A few of his students talk about wanting to "fight with the White kids after school." It sounds as though they have all located the problems in a conflict between themselves and White children who are English speakers. Emilio listens carefully to what his students have to say, trying to think of how he can turn this situation into a good learning experience.

He starts by saying, "*Para hacer su camino en este mundo tienen que ser buenos trabajando con gente muy distinta. Piensen en las diferencias humanas como realidades interesantes que nos hacen más cercanos los unos a los otros.*" ["To make your way in this world, you need to be good at working with all kinds of different people. Think about human differences as interesting realities that can bind us all more closely together."]

Some of the children shake their heads and argue with him, but Emilio encourages them to think about their problems in a positive way. He points out that they have the power to reduce conflict with words and actions, and asks, "How might you do this?" The children joke a little at first but then the discussion grows serious. They know people who have been seriously hurt in fights, and they like a lot of the children in the neighborhood and want to get along with them. The conversation moves to consideration of possible solutions to the problem.

Emilio asks all the students to write in their journals, expressing their feelings about the problems they have encountered and suggesting ways in which they might work together to support one another in the school. The next day, after reading their journals, he creates a group role-playing activity in which they have the opportunity to enact and respond to the conflicts they have experienced. The children laugh a lot as they try to role-play. At first, Emilio lets them say some silly things to loosen up. Then he keeps prodding them to really think about the best thing to say and do. After each role-play, the whole group talks about how they can form a strong classroom community to help one another deal with the problem.

Ultimately, the students decide that they will speak up for one another in a positive way when conflicts arise.

"We all belong to this school and we want to get along with everyone."
"We speak Spanish and English too; we could all do a lot of things together."
"Let's make this school better by being kind to one another."

Emilio places a box in the classroom and asks the students to write down a description of any future incidents. The whole group will take a little time daily to discuss what happened and continue to talk about ways to take a leadership role in creating better understandings and relationships.

CHILDREN AND ADVOCACY

It is important for young children to understand that good citizenship involves making a contribution to the community. They already know that there are many problems in the world and may be upset or worried about things they have seen in the media. They stand to benefit from the sense of empowerment that advocacy for others can bring. If we help children to think of themselves as activists, they can begin to develop a sense of empowerment and investment in the lives of others (Pelo & Davidson, 2000).

Children need to understand that activism is not just "helping"—it is trying to change a condition that is making life difficult for others (and possibly themselves as well). Further, we need to tell them that activism is a *collective* action that creates change when people who are concerned work together (Brunson Day, 2000). It is never too early for children to envision themselves as local and global protagonists with a commitment to a better world (Hall & Rudkin, 2011). However, children should not be made to feel responsible for solving national or world problems that are remote and complex. As activists, children can be driven by much simpler understandings and purposes than can adults, who are more weighed down by the complexities of longstanding injustice (Pelo & Davidson, 2000). We can strive for meaningful insights for our students without the burden of frightening information or unnecessary complexity.

Children do have an understanding of unfairness and hardship. They are also capable of enacting the kindness and respect for others that are natural components of activism. A good place to start is to get children interested in a school-based problem and help them to formulate some kind of engagement for the betterment of others. This is a natural extension of the democratic community—the children are already used to posing solutions to problems and taking action to be helpful and inclusive. Start with a simple problem that allows children to take as much charge as possible toward creating and implementing a solution.

Kira's Students Become Playground Activists

Kira's students have responded well to her efforts to help them get ready for their transition to 1st grade; she feels very proud of everything she has been able to do to bolster their sense of competence and self-confidence. However, she is concerned about something that happened recently. Last month was "African American History" month in her school, and her students had attended a number of assemblies focused on slavery and civil rights history. Kira had further celebrated the month by reading a number of civil rights–related books, and the children had developed a little skit on the 50th anniversary of the historic March on Washington. To her surprise, two parents later contacted her to say that their children had been upset by the assemblies and had said at home that "they did not want to be Black anymore."

Kira was very surprised by what the parents told her. She had always assumed that her young students would develop a sense of pride through the study of their history. When she thought about it more, however, she realized that some children might have become frightened or upset by the images they had seen in pictures and videos. This would have compounded any experiences they might have had previously with unkind words or actions related to racism. Kira did some research on teaching slavery to young children and realized that errors might have been made in the development of the school assemblies. The strength and resilience of the slaves over time had not been stressed; the focus on oppression and victimization must have upset the children. Kira decides that the best approach for all the children is to put the messages of the civil rights movement into action and help the children to be empowered by their own experience of activism.

Kira draws the children together and helps them recall some of the themes and events of the past month. Then she says, "You know, I think I forgot to talk to you about how strong and brave the slaves were; they were talented and skilled at many things and helped one another as much as possible. And we know how a lot of brave people of color in the civil rights movement stood up for their rights and changed laws that were not good! The pictures and videos you saw during the assembly might have frightened you; people did have a very hard time. There were bad things that happened; but let's think about everything good people were able to do by working together to change things for the better! I think that we can put our heads together and start a movement all our own. Let's think of something that you would like to make better about this school."

Many of the children immediately complain about the condition of their playground. Apparently there are tall weeds growing through some of the cracks in the cement that trip them when they run and make it hard to play games. Kira tells the children that she has a great idea: to invite the custodian to visit the next day. He comes during morning meeting and explains that, although he would like to pull the weeds, he is very busy and that is not a job that he is expected to do. However, he encourages the children to be good citizens and make the playground better for everyone. As a gift, he gives them (previously supplied by Kira) two large recycling bags for the weeds and a certificate of accomplishment that they can all sign and hang on their door after they pull the weeds.

The next week, Kira writes a little chant called "We Are Making a Playground Change" and has the children read it on a chart as they all clap. She has left space on the chart for them to plan the steps they will follow as they pull the weeds. For the next 3 days, the children spend their play time outdoors removing the weeds from the cracks in the cement. Kira takes some time after school on the last day to finish the job and puts up a small sign that says, "Playground Improvement by Kindergarten 3." As a "celebration," she and the children observe older children at recess one day to see how they are running and playing without worrying about the weeds. When they go inside, they create their "certificate of accomplishment" and hang it on the door of their classroom. Kira makes sure to stress the connection between the "playground movement" and what they learned about civil rights.

SOME PRACTICAL IDEAS FOR GETTING STARTED

Your classroom is a place where young children can begin to learn the rights and responsibilities of citizenship. Their early learning experiences will support their social and moral development, and prepare them for the interpersonal complexities of the world in which they will live. You can help them to be aware of the impact that their actions have on other people, and to see that they have the power to be a positive influence on the lives of those around them. You, the teacher, also will have the exciting opportunity to weave your own commitment to ethics, justice, and respect into the lives of your students. There are many ways in which democratic classrooms support emergent understandings of ethics, social justice, respect for diversity, and advocacy in young children. You do not need to make big changes in your classroom or purchase expensive materials; your own insightful interaction with the children and use of available (or easily obtainable) materials to prepare thoughtful lessons can go a very long way. The ideas of democracy are expansive and adaptable; most of your lessons and interactions with the children can provide you with opportunities to help children develop the skills of good citizenship.

Create More Opportunities for Talk in Your Classroom

You probably have already created many opportunities for the children to talk in your classroom. Observe carefully for a few days to see how much discussion is based on collaboration, problem solving, and resolution of conflict. You might want to plan some lessons or morning meetings with the children to expand on those important aspects of classroom conversation. If you don't have a designated place for small groups of children to sit and talk, think about creating one. Even if your day is very busy, see whether you can arrange a short meeting at the end of the day to let the children pose questions or ongoing problems for future class consideration. Post some pictures of the children in your class talking with one another, as well as some pictures of you talking with groups of children, in various parts of the classroom.

Take a Look at Your Class Rules!

If you have class rules displayed in your room, take some time to think them over. Are you satisfied with the respectful way in which they are worded? Do they help children to think about balancing their own rights with those of others? (Or do they focus mainly on obedience?) You might want to consider ways to give the children an opportunity to pose and negotiate rules related to how they should treat one another in the classroom. Give them a chance to try out the rules and evaluate their effectiveness together.

Follow the Teacher-Guides

Our teacher-guides have demonstrated multiple ways in which they help children to develop the skills of good citizenship in the classroom.

Their methods are complex and based far more on their own insights and commitments than on commercial materials or single activities. These teachers observe and listen to their students carefully; the lessons or group activities that they plan are focused on the real lives, developing skills, and understandings of their students. In some way, all of the teacher-guides have helped their children to be activists in the classroom and school. Respect for diversity is at the heart of their teaching, and their students are learning to negotiate social complexities that require conversation and respectful social relationships.

Questions for Discussion

1. What do you recall about the class rules posted in your own classrooms when you were a child? Did they help you to think about the ways in which your own actions had an impact on others in the community?
2. How might you help the children you teach to pose and negotiate their own social rules that help them to work well with one another in the classroom?
3. In what ways might you assist the children you teach to develop the skills of citizenship—continually balancing their own needs and interests with those of others?
4. How might you help your students to negotiate their own resolution of conflicts that arise in the classroom or the school?
5. What ideas do you have for helping your children to be activists who identify conditions that harm others and take collaborative steps toward making positive change?

SEVEN

The Whole World Is Waiting

Envisioning a Lifetime
of Commitment

This chapter will offer many ideas to support your long-term commitment to a career based on ethics and justice for children. It is written from the perspective that it is possible for any teacher under any circumstances to engage in purposeful and principled practice. While there is no doubt that some settings present far more challenges than others, the underlying assumption is that the determined vision of the teacher can always play a central role in the construction of outstanding service to children and to the profession.

It is only natural to become discouraged at times, so it will be important to guard against falling into "if only" thinking (if only my school had more resources, if only my administrator knew more about early childhood education, if only the parents would spend more time helping their children at home). Our "if only" thoughts probably bear much truth, but they seldom lead to improved practice. At times of discouragement, it is important to realize that it is the very things that are most lacking in our schools and the lives of the children we teach that make our commitments and advocacy so important.

We live in a society in which relatively few people gain fortune and fame; many more contribute greatly to the public good with little recognition and modest financial compensation. Teachers have long tended to be under-recognized in our society; today they are functioning heroically in the difficult context of persistent national critique. It is no wonder that some of them are questioning the value of their chosen career! Yet, without the devoted and valiant efforts of teachers, many important tasks for children would be left undone. This is why it is so important to maintain a persistent vision of strength and hope. There may be many things beyond our power, but there is *always something that we can do*. The whole world is waiting!

This book began with an emphasis on the ways in which intentionality and commitment help us to put a strong sense of purpose into daily action. Our determined focus on ethics, justice, diversity, and advocacy can define our practice in ways that support professional excellence and personal resilience. Many great possibilities always lie before us—but how can we reach our ideals in the context of the many difficult demands that we face as teachers? It is that timeless and important question that creates the need for ongoing reflection on our philosophy of teaching.

TEACHING AS A PHILOSOPHICAL JOURNEY

Our personal reasons for becoming teachers reach way back into our lives. Many different people, events, and experiences have led us into this deeply human profession. Our lives in educational institutions thus are filled with what Sarah Lawrence-Lightfoot (2004) has called "ghosts in the room"—the past experiences, relationships, and desires that have shaped us as people and professionals. There are also "ghosts" present in our philosophy of teaching, which tends to be affected by both the positive and negative memories we have of our own school experiences. We need to do the work necessary to confront our "ghosts" throughout our career and see whether any of them are interfering with our willingness to expand our thinking and incorporate new and fresh ideas.

As a beginning teacher I often complained about the "older" teachers who appeared to be getting in the way of progress. As a young witness to the revolution taking place in our nation in the 1960s, I openly shared the (ageist) belief of many peers that times were changing in ways that people who were older could not understand. (In fact, we used to say that we should not trust anyone over 30!) Now that I myself am older, I listen carefully when my young students express the same thoughts. They too complain that the "older" teachers refuse to accept new ideas or try new forms of practice. My students seem a little surprised when I suggest that our thoughts do not have to age with our bodies; that people who are older can remain enthusiastic, able to change, and open to multiple perspectives. (Conversely, I remind them that younger teachers can already be "stuck" in deficit-based or biased assumptions because they have resisted the incorporation of new ways to think about diversity. This, I suggest, might be making them "old" before their time!)

The bottom line of positive response to change is a constant willingness to revisit and revise our philosophy of teaching, with the needs of children in mind. It is inevitable that we will become more realistic, but that does not mean we must become jaded or apathetic. As brand-new teachers, for example, we might assume that children will always understand and appreciate our high expectations. We have confidence that our unflagging kindness will always help us to have positive relationships with every child. After a few years of teaching, however, we may realize that insistence on high expectations might at times appear unkind or unreasonable to some children. Possibly a child might sulk for an entire day after being encouraged to redo some aspects of a small project. (And we might later discover that, in her culture, it is shameful to be asked to redo completed work.)

Such an event should challenge us to revisit our philosophy to include several emergent complexities. We now have a greater sense of the need for patience and forgiveness, and we also see that we must always leave room for cultural misunderstandings about the high expectations we hold. Further, it is now clear that our determination to be kind and positive must transcend the small and large conflicts that emerge and must be resolved in the classroom. A refreshing change to our philosophy in the context of the above experience would require a sense of humility and a willingness to recognize and act on the shortcomings of our current system of belief. It would indicate that we can retain our ideals while adjusting our ideas to incorporate new understandings and experiences.

A very different response would be the negative conclusion that "kids like these just don't want to work hard." We sometimes do hear this kind of comment in schools—and, yes, sometimes from the older teachers. But we all need to guard against such thoughts. If we focus on our dedication to the children and accept that fact that all ideas inevitably need to change over time, it is entirely possible to retain a lively and enthusiastic professional stance throughout our careers.

Kira Revises Her Educational Philosophy

Kira has felt herself changing in positive ways during her first year as a public school kindergarten teacher. She has been thinking quite a bit about her studies in philosophy as an undergraduate and the ways in which they led her to an alternative teacher preparation program. In her senior year of college, Kira decided that she wanted to find some way to apply all the philosophy she had learned to a real-life situation; a number of her professors encouraged her to take advantage of a prestigious federally funded alternative teacher preparation program at a nearby university to gain teacher certification. Kira was not sure that she wanted to be a career teacher, but she was eager to learn about education and get experience teaching children.

Kira really enjoyed teaching her kindergarten students but she had been frustrated with what she saw as the discriminatory forces that seemed to work against them in the school. She had become friendly with a few teachers but the librarian with whom she had spoken about the problematic punishment situation was socially cool toward her now. Some other teachers were polite but distant. Kira knew that several of her best friends in the alternative teacher preparation program had already decided to leave the classroom; most of them were entering graduate studies in other fields. She herself had considered leaving teaching at one point during the year but quickly decided against it. Kira was hooked—she loved teaching and she did not want to leave her students behind.

When Kira's principal offered to renew her position for another year she readily agreed. But she also talked with him for a while about some of her concerns. His response was friendly but direct; he told her that teaching and working with other teachers to support all her students would never be easy. If she wanted to make a difference, he said, she would have to "take the heat." Driving home after that meeting, Kira realized that her whole future career probably would involve some of the tensions and difficulties she had experienced in her first year.

Thinking things over further, Kira felt very comfortable with her creativity in the classroom. It was good to know that she had been able to implement many of the ideas from her preparation program; she was especially proud of the library exhibit she had arranged. The "movement" to clean the weeds from the playground had left her exhilarated—the children really seemed to grow in confidence through that activity. It was not easy for Kira to be assertive with the library teacher, but she still believed that it was very important to address that situation.

Ultimately, Kira decided that it was her philosophical approach to conflict and frustration that needed to change. She had been somewhat intimidated by others and had spent too much time at home fretting over the ways in which some of the teachers talked about and treated the children in the transitional kindergarten. With a successful year of teaching behind her, Kira decided that she would expand her philosophy to include acknowledgment of the persistent challenges inherent in standing up for children in schools. She was determined to retain her enthusiasm and good nature as well as her commitment to equal treatment for her students.

Kira had requested the transitional kindergarten again for next year and was determined to find as many ways as possible to set a positive tone and work collaboratively with other teachers to help them see the potential in her students. She was convinced that her advocacy for the children could make a real difference; she now accepted that some days of doubt and tension were going to be inevitable. She was determined to become a leader within the school.

THE IMPORTANCE OF TEACHER LEADERSHIP

Some years ago, I watched a television interview with a former teacher who had just been appointed president of a prestigious university. When asked about her journey from the classroom to the presidency, the newly appointed president indicated that she had decided to do more with her life than "just teach." Thus, she left the classroom to seek greater avenues of power and influence on the university level.

I have reflected many times on these comments, and I think they bear close examination. My own preference is that the word *just* would never appear in front of the word *teach*. Teaching is a highly specialized undertaking in and of itself. It stands alone as a distinguished career with specified skills and qualifications. Those who choose to teach do powerful work with unique outcomes that cannot be replicated or improved upon in different career choices. Thus, I would argue that the college president being interviewed really had decided to do "something else." While we are all free to make career moves, I would assert that making new choices should not diminish the inherent value and importance of teaching as a lifelong career.

Teaching Is a Unique Professional Undertaking

Possibly my support of the distinguished nature of teaching appears naïve, considering the almost unlimited criticism currently being unleashed against teachers in the United States. There can be no doubt that the position of college president is a highly responsible one that carries far more prestige and financial benefit than classroom teaching. Yet, the outcomes of the college presidency and those of classroom teaching are worlds apart. Teachers live in close daily relationship with a small group of children; they have an intimate opportunity to touch the lives of their students in very powerful ways.

Almost everyone I ask can recall the names of their elementary school teachers from kindergarten up; they consider their memories of these teachers to be important. This reinforces my recognition of the enduring impact of the *relationships* that teachers forge with their students—an impact often ignored by critics focusing only on the scores of standardized tests. It is in these close daily relationships that teachers demonstrate the personal integrity and professional expertise necessary to meet the ever-increasing demands being placed upon them. Teachers can never rest behind their Internet image or public relations strategies; they share the fundamental essence of who they are and what they know in close contact with others every day.

Teachers Can Be Leaders

The good news is that teachers do not have to leave their classrooms or become school administrators in order to be *leaders* in their schools.

Rather they can aspire to be teacher leaders who model their commitments and skills through strong collaborative relationships with professional peers. Educational researchers and policymakers are increasing their call for teacher leadership because teachers have intimate knowledge of schools, children, and curriculum. They "speak the language" of teaching and have credibility with their peers. The decision to embrace the identity of teacher leader gives teachers the opportunity to retain their commitment to classroom teaching while having a greater influence on their schools. The title teacher leader can be formal or informal; any teacher can aspire to embrace a stronger leadership role in her or his daily work (Lieberman & Friedrich, 2010).

Aanetra's Leadership Opportunity

Aanetra has had a very interesting year in the pre-K program in her public school. Her initial "What's in a Name" workshop with the parents seemed to have a good impact, as did her subsequent workshop on the importance of play and inclusion in early childhood. Some of the parents have been volunteering in her room, and she also sees that more of the parents are talking to one another before and after school. Aanetra's talent for working with parents has been noticed by her principal and early childhood supervisor. She recently has been offered the opportunity to be the parent-community liaison for her program.

Aanetra has thought about this opportunity carefully, and it seems like a big responsibility. She will be released from her classroom 1 day a week to consult with teachers about family engagement in the program. She will also offer a number of parent workshops throughout the next year. There is modest funding for her position in the federal grant. As she is considering the offer, she is quietly approached by an experienced teacher in the building. "Watch out," this teacher says, "because they are going to give you a little bit of money and expect you to still be responsible for your classroom and do a lot of extra work." Aanetra talks with the other teacher more and explains how exciting it has been to see the positive impact of working with the parents.

Aanetra talks with her supervisors and expresses concern about leaving her classroom for a day a week. Her principal assures her that the substitute position has been offered to one of her former student teachers and that it will be permanent for the year. Aanetra is happy about this, as it also will give her a good chance to mentor her excellent former student. Ultimately, she decides to accept the opportunity. The first thing she is planning is a new workshop for the parents on understanding the value of inclusion in the early childhood classroom. She hopes to engage several of her colleagues in her workshops throughout the coming year.

Collaborative Professional Communities

It is natural for early childhood educators who foster democratic practices in their classrooms to extend these practices to their work with colleagues. The ideal of schools as collaborative professional communities rests on the idea that teachers can support and inform one another in meaningful ways. Such collaboration is closely related to the concept of participatory advocacy; teacher leaders should not hesitate to express their ideas and try to influence the beliefs and practices of their colleagues. It is also possible for teacher leaders to play a more formal role in the professional development of their peers or in the mentoring of new teachers. In an endless variety of ways, teacher leaders effectively extend the commitments they have embraced in a way that constructs a sense of community and shared purpose with colleagues. They find many ways to make commitments to ethics, justice, respect for diversity, and advocacy accessible to as many professionals as possible.

Teachers in any given educational setting are diverse in terms of background and professional preparation. One of the important tasks for teacher leaders is to contribute to a cohesive professional community while respecting differences of perspective and opinion. This calls for the often delicate balance of negotiating a sense of common purpose in the context of discourse that honors divergent ideas (Kanpol, 1998).

Calling the Question

The sense of professional solidarity constructed by teacher leaders can help colleagues to look at some hard facts in the workplace. In their book *Ready or Not: Leadership Choices in Early Care and Education,* authors Stacie Goffin and Valora Washington (2007) indicate that it is time to call the question about professional responsibility. By this they mean, among other things, that we as early childhood professionals must confront resistance to follow the knowledge base about what is good for children. Our teacher-guide Aanetra was effective in calling the question, for example, when she argued against the idea of focusing more on academic skills for the children who seemed more advanced in her pre-K program. She reminded her supervisor and administrator about both the importance of the play-based curriculum and the program's central goal of inclusion.

Goffin and Washington also urge us to have the integrity to call the poor performance of colleagues into question. This can be difficult in any setting, even in a university setting where faculty have the contractual responsibility for peer review. We teachers tend to be kind and nurturing people; it can be quite difficult to confront colleagues whose performance appears to be less than adequate. While it is usually administrators who are charged with evaluating teacher performance in schools and programs, teacher leaders can help in a variety of ways.

For example, shared conversations about explicit expectations for practice among colleagues can open the door to reflection. Also, providing avenues for teachers to demonstrate their best practices gives everyone in the school an opportunity to see examples of excellence. There are times, however, when it is necessary for teachers to address issues of concern with colleagues. Our teacher-guide Kira did this when she felt that the library teacher had been unfair and unkind to her students. As long as we keep the needs of children front and center, and treat colleagues with respect and compassion, true benefits can come from a positive approach to confronting issues of professional competence.

Jordan Calls the Question About Diversity

Jordan has become increasingly aware of the need to introduce his students to many different forms of diversity. He started the year concerned about deficit views of rural life and initiated some ways for all the teachers in the center to articulate the positive aspects of the geographical lives of the children. The revision of his farm unit to help the children be familiar with forms of social activism seemed to work very well; he has continued to help the children get a sense of the importance of contributing to one's community. More recently, he has been preparing the children for the diversities with which they are less familiar and that they will encounter when they bus to the regional elementary school for 1st grade. In the process of this latest initiative, Jordan has become much more aware of some challenges that must be addressed.

It is clear that some of the children have been exposed to negative views of diversity in their homes. Apparently some families have expressed disparaging views of the migrant workers who sometimes work on their farms or live in the community. It is also clear that some children have been exposed to negative views of people with darker skin color; Jordan overhears prejudiced talk among some children near the interactive bulletin board. Jordan has talked with a few of his colleagues about his concerns; they seem uncomfortable with the subject. The center director has appeared to skirt the issue as well—the topic of diversity rarely if ever comes up in faculty meetings or discussions.

Jordan knows from his visit to the elementary school that the children are going to need to develop stronger cultural competence before they start 1st grade. He also knows that they will be living their adult lives in a global society and wants them to have comprehensive opportunities to become more culturally competent. As he thinks about it, he believes the center needs to institute a comprehensive diversity initiative. Jordan sees this as central to good educational practice and responsible preparation for the future.

At the next faculty meeting, Jordan raises the topic of diversity as an important issue for consideration. Some faculty members disagree with his concerns; they liked his former initiative about the positives of rural living but think it would "create trouble" to try to address diversities that are not in the community. Jordan reminds everyone about the increasing kinds of diversity he observed during his visit to the elementary school.

One of the other teachers, whom Jordan does not know well, speaks up to mention that a small diversity grant currently is being offered to child-care centers through a national professional organization. She offers to work with Jordan to apply for the grant, which would pay for books, films, and other resources related to diversity. Jordan takes her up on her offer, and the director suggests that a small committee be formed to focus on diversity curriculum in the center. Two other teachers volunteer. Some of the other teachers continue to express the idea that a diversity project is unnecessary, but Jordan is happy that he and other teachers can begin to work to move forward on this important initiative.

Formal and Informal Teacher Leadership

Some programs and school districts have official teacher leader designations; possibly grade leaders or subject area "coaches" (such as reading coaches). Where such designations do not exist (and even where they do), you do not need permission or special certification to "assign yourself" to important aspects of teacher leadership. You simply might decide to model collegiality and helpfulness, opening your door to peers who need assistance or advice. Or, like our teacher-guides, you might include relationship building with other teachers as part of enhancing the perception of your students within the school building.

You also can refuse to use disparaging language about children regardless of ability or background, and model positive words that value and uphold respect for children. The participatory advocacy discussed in this book offers many opportunities for teacher leadership. Simply modeling willingness to speak up at faculty meetings and express opinions may help others to begin to do so. You can always seek to share your own areas of professional growth with others. The best way for you to learn more about becoming a teacher leader is to take some steps to become one in your school or program.

REACHING OUT TO HONOR FAMILY EMOTIONS AND EXPERIENCE

The leadership and advocacy of teachers inevitably extend into the lives of families and others in the community. While this chapter does not allow the space for an extensive examination of family and community involvement, it is important to emphasize that our commitments can and should guide us to extend respect and understanding to all the adults who are important to the children in our classrooms. Our teacher-guide Aanetra has provided an example of reaching out to engage parents and help them to think about issues related to their children in school. Emilio also provided an example of a teacher who needed to come to terms with his personal feelings about the sexual orientation of a parent and to make plans to get to know the parent and his partner better. Another example was provided by Kira, who reached out into the community to find out more about the housing in which the children lived; she took steps to create more respect for them and their neighborhood through her library display. Jordan invited a local farmer to his classroom and engaged the students in a project related to the agriculture that was central to community life. All of these initiatives were characterized by the desire of the teachers to honor communities and families, and to strengthen relationships in ways that enhanced opportunities for children in the classroom.

I recently reread Sarah Lawrence-Lightfoot's insightful book *The Essential Conversation: What Parents and Teachers Can Learn from Each Other* (2004). Toward the beginning of this book, Dr. Lawrence-Lightfoot recounts the story of the day when her 2nd-grade teacher Mrs. Sullivan informed her African American parents (as she stood listening) that she was probably not "college material." Even as a child she knew that her teacher was wrong, and she looked to her usually outspoken parents to counter what Mrs. Sullivan was saying. To her surprise, they demurred and stayed silent. Only later did she understand that her parents were afraid to speak. They knew that a teacher had the power to do great harm to a child, and their desire to protect her was foremost in their minds. Even later in life, when she believed her own daughter was experiencing subtle abuse from a teacher, Dr. Lawrence-Lightfoot's mother cautioned her to be careful and not to put her daughter in danger by antagonizing the teacher.

It is almost incredible to place this story in the context of the remarkable achievements of Dr. Lawrence-Lightfoot's parents. Her mother was a renowned pediatrician and child psychiatrist, and her father was an eminent sociologist and activist—a former student of W.E.B. Du Bois. Dr. Lawrence-Lightfoot ultimately became renowned in her own right as a

Harvard-based educator and sociologist. We have to wonder how many times we as teachers may have interpreted similar family silences as "not caring about education" or "not being involved." Could the parents have been afraid of us and of the power we had over their child? This troubling possibility should be the impetus for careful reflection on our judgments of parents and our interpretations of their reluctance to become involved in schools. It also challenges us to think ethically about our words and assumptions when speaking to parents about their children.

It is essential for us to share our expertise without seeming to subordinate the knowledge of parents (MacNaughton, 2003). If we find ways to touch the wellspring of parental understanding and love, we can open up creative spaces for positive and informative two-way communication. This requires a form of "skilled dialogue" (p. xix) characterized by *respect* (acknowledgment that perspectives are equally valued), *reciprocity* (intent to support multiple perspectives), and *response* (communication of empathy even in the absence of agreement with all perspectives) (Barrera & Corso, 2003). This is an approach to discourse with parents and families that can ease fear and help us to be compassionate and open-minded as we open our minds to important new perspectives. Such perspectives can do a great deal to strengthen our advocacy for the students in our care.

When I reflect on the concepts of skilled dialogue, I remember a mother who came to school to meet with me one afternoon. I had been talking with the children in my class about the importance of trying to resolve problems without fighting, and her son went home and told his mother that his teacher said it was wrong to fight. She said, "Mrs. Fennimore, I have tried in the past to go along with what you teachers tell our kids about fighting. But our kids live in this neighborhood, and you teachers do not. I encouraged my first son not to fight. He became the target for every bully in the neighborhood and got hurt a lot. Now I tell my little boy to fight and fight fast. That will settle the problem, and he will be safer because he will not become a target. The other kids will respect him and know he can fight back."

I had a lot to learn from this mother, and from her perspective. I continue to share her words when I discuss parent involvement in my classes as well as in professional development with teachers. They embody a dilemma that many teachers confront; fighting as an issue is not as clear-cut as we initially might think! What about the children for whom fighting may be a matter of staying safe? Or even staying alive? We do not have to agree with the position of the parent, but we have the obligation to understand her perspective and include it in our thinking about a complex dilemma.

Emilio Reaches Out to Support a Parent Struggle

Emilio has worked hard this year to support his bilingual students and to help prepare them for their transition to the older elementary grades. The students seemed to gain a lot from their language heritage projects and their increased interaction with other students in the school. They are all still very proud of the letter from the library attesting to the importance of their public service. Recently, as he stood at the doorway of the school to say good-bye to students as they exited, he was approached by the leader of the Parent Teacher Association (PTA) in the school. She said she had heard a rumor that the school board was considering limiting bilingual education in the district to kindergarten and 1st grade only. Emilio doubted that this rumor was true, but promised to check into it.

The next day, when he asked his principal, Emilio found out that initial discussions of limiting bilingual education to early grades were indeed taking place in district offices. Several members of the school board felt strongly that starting English-only classes earlier might help the children to get higher scores on standardized tests. Emilio felt angry and let down; he asked his principal what he might be able to do to encourage the school board not to make this change. The principal indicated that the teachers' union was already involved and that Emilio should contact his representatives as soon as possible. Further, he indicated that Emilio might talk with some PTA parents to encourage them to communicate with the school board about the issue.

Emilio went to the next PTA meeting, which was attended by a few parents. He explored the emergent bilingual issue and informed the parents of the procedure for becoming registered speakers at the next school board meeting. The parents indicated discomfort and fear about being involved in any public hearings. Emilio understood their feelings, but he encouraged them to gather their courage together and think about the future of their younger children and other children in the community. *"Tienen que pensar de sí mismos como expertos en sus hijos/as y su comunidad. Ustedes tienen el derecho de hacerle preguntas a los que dirigen las escuelas y ustedes tienen el derecho de obtener respuestas. Sus hijos/as cuentan con ustedes."* ["You need to think of yourselves as experts on your children and your community. You have the right to ask questions of those who run the schools, and you have the right to get answers. Your children are counting on you."]

ADVOCACY IN THE MORAL TERRAIN

In his book *Moral Outrage in Education,* author David Purpel (2005) reminded us that educators inevitably move beyond the school doors and into important moral terrains. As teachers, we see all the complex dilemmas that affect our students and their families. Thus, as compassionate and caring human beings, we are compelled to respond in meaningful ways to the continuing discriminatory nature of race, class, and gender and other relationships in the United States. Likewise, we are called to respond with compassion to the economic realities that leave some children experiencing homelessness, food insecurity, and untreated medical and dental maladies. Poverty and discrimination cause unnecessary suffering in the lives of many children and their families.

Our moral outrage should not paralyze us—we should be propelled instead toward a society characterized by social justice. At the very least, this should be a society that protects all children by ensuring that their basic needs for survival are met. Schools cannot by themselves solve all the problems we and our students face in the days and years ahead. However, schools can make a significant contribution to a good and just world (Purpel, 1989)—and each of us can play an important role in that contribution.

SOME FINAL THOUGHTS ON ADVOCACY

A parent (also an experienced preschool teacher) has enrolled her oldest child in her local urban public school. The parent is committed to the democratic principles embedded in public education and wants her child to experience many forms of diversity in her school. Over the past 2 years of kindergarten and 1st grade, the parent has become increasingly aware of discriminatory attitudes toward some children in the school. Many of the children are poor; there are also many children of color and children who are recent immigrants. She realizes that more affluent and prestigious White parents are accustomed to special treatment; they successfully negotiate for the placement of their children in the "top classes" with the "best teachers." She also has heard a vice principal and a few teachers refer to the "top kids" as the "only good kids in the school." This concerns her a great deal.

When it is almost time for her second child to be enrolled in kindergarten, the parent receives information from the private preschool in which that child is enrolled about a new gifted program in the school district. This new program is located in the wealthiest community in the school district, and information is being distributed only to parents whose children are in private schools. Parents must pay $100 to the school district for their children to be tested for the program; they are assured that their children will be placed in a separate section of the school and will receive many added resources, including small class size, unlimited use of buses for trips, and paraprofessionals in every classroom.

The parent is concerned about the fairness of this program on a number of levels (there are already designated gifted classes in other schools in the district that have large classes and receive no extra funding) and raises questions about it with other school parents. A few of them decide to ask for a meeting with the district superintendent about gifted services in the district. During the meeting they are warned that asking questions about the new program may "get them into trouble"—the superintendent tells them that the parents of the children now in the first year of the new gifted program are politically connected, very organized, and outspoken.

Some of the parents present at the meeting soon withdraw from the group, but a few persist and subsequently testify at a school board meeting to raise questions about gifted services for all children. They specifically request a district policy statement on gifted education indicating how all parents will be informed of the existence of the new program at kindergarten registration, how all qualified children will have fair access to affordable testing, and how all qualified children will be equally served.

To the immense surprise of the parent who initiated the questions about the gifted program, this public request to the school board started a highly publicized political firestorm that lasted almost 2 years. At its height, the local newspaper (which usually had one or two letters to the editor) placed a large number of letters it had received about the gifted program on the first four pages of a special edition. The parents of children in the gifted program publicly castigated the small group of parents who had raised questions as "destroyers of services for gifted children." At one packed and angry school board meeting, a parent from the gifted program called his child a "fine steak" and referred to the students in the regular classes as "garbage." Neither the superintendent nor any member of the school board present commented on or countered that statement.

Ultimately, there were positive outcomes of the initiative. The school board provided a policy statement on gifted education, and a notice about the program was posted in every school. Free testing was available in the district for children recommended for the program, and the program was expanded to several other sites. However, there were still important questions remaining about equal recognition of child giftedness and equal access to the program. Over 20 years later, a publication of the Bar Association in that city raised the same questions about gifted services that initially had been raised by the group of parents in this school district.

I was the urban public school parent who initiated this controversy, and it was my first (not my last) encounter with the realities of equity-related advocacy initiatives. An extended narrative of this and another urban equity initiative in which I became deeply involved can be read in my article "Brown and the Failure of Civic Responsibility" (Fennimore,

2005). Suffice it to say that any naiveté I might have had about what happens when advocates stand up against forces that privilege some children and oppress others was permanently erased. Those were tough fights; they took a lot of time and the ultimate gains were not as extensive as I would have wished. However, I've never doubted the value and importance of standing up and speaking out as I did. My work with other parents and citizens opened my eyes to the incredible challenges faced by advocates for children, and served to center my commitments and determination to stand up for children throughout my career.

Real-World Teacher Activism

Considering the above scenario, it might seem that examples of teacher advocacy in this book are somewhat mild and conciliatory. The hypothetical teacher-guides, for example, are not openly confrontational with administrators or other teachers. They try to help their students, to interrupt harmful circumstances, and to raise the consciousness of others—without unnecessarily antagonizing anyone. I like to think of these teacher-guides as courageous and peace-oriented; their passion for advocacy is strong but professionally contained. The teacher-guides do not back down from their commitments, but they maintain relationships that are as positive and productive as possible with others. All four of them want very much to continue to teach successfully in their schools; they are not acting in ways so radical as to put their employment or continued professional success in jeopardy.

I think it is very important to recognize that outspoken school parents, community citizens, and professionals who are employed as advocates are acting under far fewer constraints than classroom teachers who want to be advocates in their own schools. I accepted the considerable controversy (and hostility) that I encountered as an advocate for public school equity, but my citizen-based activism did not put my professional employment in jeopardy. In fact, I believe it added considerably to the quality of my writing and teaching. While I am definitely outspoken and positioned in my professional workplace, obviously I also have maintained the positive relationships necessary to become a tenured and fully promoted professor.

I think it is essential to acknowledge that all advocates must make some compromises, particularly when their families are counting on them for long-term economic support. That is why I have made every attempt in this book to respect the realities of teachers and to open spaces for effective but reasonable activism. I have tried to construct the teacher-guides as outstanding and dedicated professionals who are moving daily toward teacher leadership and sustained advocacy. They want to be good employees and successful teachers as well as advocates; their success is going to make a big difference in the lives of children.

Stay Focused on Your Commitments!

That being said, hopefully we all do and will have the courage to stand up, speak out, and act with adequate force when our commitments and our conscience require us to do so. All things in life must be balanced; with continued persistence and vision I believe we all can find a constructive balance between personal responsibility, career success, and effective child advocacy. Never give up on your ethics, your sense of justice, your respect for diversity, or your determination to be an advocate. There is always a way to fit your commitments into your daily practice. All the children depend on us; the whole world is waiting!

References

Applebaum, B. (2009). Is teaching for social justice a liberal bias? *Teachers College Record, 111*(2), 376–408.

Austin, J. L. (1962). *How to do things with words.* Oxford, UK: University of Oxford Press.

Ayers, W., Kumashiro, K., Meiners, E., Quinn, T., & Stovall, D. (2010). *Teaching toward democracy: Educators as agents of change.* Boulder, CO: Paradigm.

Bakhtin, M. M. (1986). *Speech genres & other late essays.* Austin, TX: University of Texas.

Bakhtin, M. M. (1993). *Toward a philosophy of the act.* Austin, TX: University of Texas Press.

Banks, J. A. (2007a). *Educating citizens in a multicultural society* (2nd ed.). New York, NY: Teachers College Press.

Banks, J. A. (2007b). Series foreword. In S. H. Alim & J. Baugh (Eds.), *Talkin black talk: Language, education, and social change* (pp. ix–xiii). New York, NY: Teachers College Press.

Banks, J. A., & Banks, C. M. (1995). *Handbook of research on multicultural education.* Boston, MA: Jossey-Bass.

Barrera, I., & Corso, R. (2003). *Skilled dialogue: Strategies for responding to cultural diversity in early childhood.* Baltimore, MD: Paul H. Brookes.

Bender-Slack, D., & Raupach, M. P. (2008). Negotiating standards and social justice in social studies: Educators' perspectives. *Social Studies, 99*(6), 255–259.

Berk, L. E., & Winsler, A. (1995). *Scaffolding children's learning: Vygotsky and early childhood education.* Washington, DC: National Association for Early Childhood Education.

Bourdieu, P. (1991). *Language and symbolic power* (J. B. Thompson, Ed., G. Raymond & M. Adamson, Trans.). Cambridge, MA: Harvard University Press.

Bourdieu, P., & Passeron, J. C. (1990). *Reproduction in education, society, and culture.* Los Angeles, CA: Sage.

Boutte, G. S. (2008). Beyond the illusion of diversity: How early childhood teachers can promote social justice. *Social Studies, 99*(4), 165–173.

Brazelton, T. B. (1990, September 9). Why is America failing its children? *The New York Times*, p. SM41.

Brunson Day, C. (2000). Foreword. In A. Pelo & F. Davidson (Eds.), *That's not fair: A teacher's guide to activism for young children* (pp. x–xi). St. Paul, MN: Redleaf Press.

Campbell, E. (2003). *The ethical teacher.* Berkshire, UK: Open University Press.

Carlton, M. P., & Winsler, A. (1999). School readiness: The need for a paradigm shift. *School Psychology Review, 28*(3), 338–352.

Castagno, A. E. (2009). Making sense of multicultural education: A synthesis of various typologies found in the literature. *Multicultural Perspectives, 11*(1), 43–48.

Children's Defense Fund. (2011). *State of America's children 2010.* Available at www.childrensdefense.org/child-research-data-publications/data/state-of-americas-children-2010-report.html

Children's Defense Fund. (2013). *Children in the United States.* Available at www.childrensdefense.org/child-research-data-publications/data/state-data-repository/cits/2013/2013-united-states-children-in-the-states.pdf

Cohen, J. L. (2010). Teachers in the news: A critical analysis of one newspaper's discourse in education. *Discourse: Studies in the Cultural Politics of Education, 31*(1), 105–119.

Coles, R. (1997). *The moral intelligence of children.* New York, NY: Random House.

Cummins, J. (1989). *Empowering minority students.* Sacramento, CA: California Association for Bilingual Education.

Cunningham, M. (1990, October 7). Why America fails its children. *The New York Times,* p. SM41.

Daily, S., Burkhauser, M., & Halle, T. (2011). School readiness practices in the United States. *National Civic Review, 100*(4), 21–24.

Danforth, S., & Gabel, S. (2006).*Vital questions facing disability studies in education.* New York, NY: Peter Lang.

Darling-Hammond, L. (2012). Foreword. In B. Falk (Ed.), *Defending childhood: Keeping the promise of early education* (pp. vii–ix). New York, NY: Teachers College Press.

De Gaetano, Y. (2011). Education that is multicultural and promotes social justice. In B. S. Fennimore & A. L. Goodwin (Eds.), *Promoting social justice for young children* (pp. 71–80). New York, NY: Springer.

De Graaf, J. (2005) Childhood affluenza. In A. G. Cosby, R. E. Greenberg, L. H. Southward, & M. Weitzman (Eds.), *About children* (pp. 1–12). Elk Grove Village, IL: American Academy of Pediatrics.

Derman-Sparks, L., & A.B.C. Task Force. (1989). *Anti-bias curriculum: Tools for empowering young children.* Washington, DC: National Association for the Education of Young Children.

Derman-Sparks, L., & Ramsey, P. G. (2006). *What if all the kids are white: Anti-bias multicultural education with young children and families.* New York, NY: Teachers College Press.

DeVries, R., & Zan, B. (1994). *Moral classrooms, moral children: Creating a constructivist atmosphere in early education.* New York, NY: Teachers College Press.

Dombro, A. L., Jablon, J., & Stetson, C. (2011). *How to connect with children to extend their learning.* Washington, DC: National Association for the Education of Young Children.

Dudley-Marling, C. (2007). Return of the deficit. *Journal of Educational Controversy,* 2(1), n.p.

Durac, L. (2011). Ethics, a basis in the formation of the moral character of the educated individual in the knowledge society. *Journal of US–China Public Administration, 8*(10), 1136–1141.

Espinosa, L. M., Thornburg, K. R., & Matthews, M. C. (1997). Rural kindergarten teachers' perceptions of school readiness: A comparison with the Carnegie Study. *Early Childhood Education Journal, 25*(2), 119–126.

Feeney, S., & Freeman, N. K. (2005). *Ethics and the early childhood educator: Using the NAEYC code,* (2nd ed.). Washington, DC: National Association for the Education of Young Children.

Fennimore, B. S. (1989). *Child advocacy for early childhood educators.* New York, NY: Teachers College Press.

Fennimore, B. S. (2000). *Talk matters: Refocusing the language of public schooling.* New York, NY: Teachers College Press.

Fennimore, B. S. (2005). Brown and the failure of civic responsibility. *Teachers College Record, 5*(107), 1905–1932.

Fennimore, B. S. (2007). Know where you stand and stand there: Everyday advocacy for children of diversity. *Childhood Education, 83*(3), 294–299.

Fennimore, B. S. (2008). Talk about children: Developing a living curriculum of advocacy and social justice. In C. Genishi & A. L. Goodwin (Eds.), *Diversities in early childhood education: Rethinking and doing* (pp. 185–200). New York, NY: Routledge.

Fennimore, B. S. (2011). The continuing struggle for social justice for children. In B. S. Fennimore & A. L. Goodwin (Eds.), *Promoting social justice for young children* (pp. 1–7). New York, NY: Springer.

Ferri, B. A., & Bacon, J. (2011). Beyond inclusion: Disability studies in early childhood teacher education. In B. S. Fennimore & A. L. Goodwin (Eds.), *Promoting social justice for young children* (pp. 137–146). New York, NY: Springer.

Fine, M. (1993). Making controversy: Who's at risk? In R. Wollons (Ed.), *Children at risk in America: History, concepts, and public policy* (pp. 91–110). Albany, NY: State University of New York Press.

Forni, P. M. (2002). *Choosing civility: The twenty-five rules of considerate conduct.* New York, NY: St. Martin's Griffin.

Fullan, M., & Hargreaves, A. (1998). *What's worth fighting for out there?* New York, NY: Teachers College Press.

Garbarino, J. (1995). *Raising children in a socially toxic environment.* San Francisco, CA: Jossey-Bass.

Garcia, K. (2002). Swimming against the mainstream: Examining cultural assumptions in the classroom. In L. Darling-Hammond, J. French, & S. P. Garcia-Lopez (Eds.), *Learning to teach for social justice* (pp. 22–29). New York, NY: Teachers College Press.

Gesell, A., & Ilg, F. L. (1943). *Infant and child in the culture of today.* New York, NY: Harpers.

Giovacco-Johnson, T. (2011). Applied ethics as a foundation in early childhood teacher education. *Early Childhood Education Journal, 38*(6), 449–456.

Goffin, S. G., & Lombardi, J. (1988). *Speaking out: Early childhood advocacy.* Washington, DC: National Association for the Education of Young Children.

Goffin, S. G., & Washington, V. (2007). *Ready or not: Leadership choices in early care and education.* New York, NY: Teachers College Press.

Goffman, E. (1959). *The presentation of self in everyday life.* New York, NY: Doubleday.

Hall, E. L. & Rudkin, J. K. (2011). *Seen and heard: Children's rights in early childhood education.* New York: Teachers College Press.

Haydon, G. (2006). *Education philosophy and the ethical environment.* New York, NY: Routledge.

Head, N. (2008). Critical theory and its practices: Habermas, Kosovo, and international relations. *Politics, 23*(3), 150–159.

Hopkins, W. E. (1997). *Ethical dimensions of diversity.* Thousand Oaks, CA: Sage.

Johns, B. H., McGrath, M. Z., & Mather, S. R. (2008). *Ethical dilemmas in education: Standing up for honesty and integrity.* Lanham, MD: R & L Education.

Johnson, M. A., & Stephens, M. L. (2012). Race to the top and exclusion of welfare recipients from educational policy discourse. *Adult Learning, 23*(4), 188–195.

Johnston, P. (2004). *Choice words: How our language affects children's learning.* Portland, ME: Stenhouse.

Kanpol, B. (1998). *Teachers talking back and breaking bread.* Cresskill, NJ: Hampton Press.

Keith-Spiegel, P., Whitley, B. E., Balogh, D. W., Perkins, D. V., & Whittig, A. F. (2002). *The ethics of teaching: A casebook* (2nd ed.). Mahwah, NJ: Erlbaum.

King, J. E. (1991). Dysconscious racism: Ideology, identity, and the miseducation of teachers. *Journal of Negro Education, 60*(2), 133–146.

Kohl, H. (2000). Teaching for social justice. *Rethinking Schools, 15*(2), n.p.

Koppelman, K. (2011). *The great diversity debate: Embracing pluralism in school and society.* New York, NY: Teachers College Press.

La Paro, K. M., & Pianta, R. (2000). Kindergarten teachers' reported use of kindergarten to first grade transition practices. *Elementary School Journal, 101*(1), 63–79.

Ladson-Billings, G. (1995). Toward a theory of culturally relevant pedagogy. *American Educational Research Journal, 32*(3), 465–491.

Ladson-Billings, G. (2009). *The dream keepers: Successful teachers of African American children.* San Francisco, CA: Jossey-Bass.

Laman, T. T., Miller, E. T., & Lopez-Robertson, J. (2012). Noticing and naming as social practice: Examining the relevance of a contextualized field-based early childhood literacy methods course. *Journal of Early Childhood Teacher Education, 33*(1), 3–18.

Lara-Cinisomo, S., Fuligni, A., Ritchie, S., Howes, C., & Karoly, L. (2008). Getting ready for school: An examination of early childhood educators' belief systems. *Early Childhood Education Journal, 35*(4), 343–349.

Lawrence-Lightfoot, S. (2004). *The essential conversation: What parents and teachers can learn from each other.* New York, NY: Ballantine Books.

Levin, D. E. (2003). *Teaching young children in violent times: Building a peaceable classroom* (2nd ed.). Cambridge, MA: Educators for Social Responsibility with National Association for the Education of Young Children.

Levin, D. E. (2011). Objectified self, objectified relationships: The sexualization of childhood promotes social injustice. In B. S. Fennimore & A. L. Goodwin (Eds.), *Promoting social justice for young children* (pp. 25–34). New York, NY: Springer.

Lewit, E. M., & Baker, S. L. (1995). School readiness. *The Future of Children, 5*(2), 128–139.

Lieberman, A., & Friedrich, L. D. (2010). *How teachers become leaders: Learning from practice and research.* New York, NY: Teachers College Press.

Luthar, S., & Barkin, S. H. (2012). Are affluent youth truly "at risk"? Vulnerability and resiliency across three samples. *Development and Psychology, 24*(2), 429–449.

Macdonald, M. B. (2011). Preface. In B. S. Fennimore & A. L. Goodwin (Eds.), *Promoting social justice for young children* (pp. xii–viii). New York, NY: Springer.

MacKinnon, C. A. (1992). *Only words.* Cambridge, MA: Harvard University Press.

MacNaughton, G. (2003). *Shaping early childhood: Learners, curriculum, and contexts.* Berkshire, UK: Open University Press.

Maxwell, K. L., & Clifford, R. M. (2004). School readiness assessment. *Beyond the journal: Young children on the web.* Available at journal.naeyc.org/btj/200401/Maxwell.pdf

Murray, T. R. (2008). *God in the classroom.* Lanham, MD: R & L Education.

National Association for the Education of Young Children. (2011). *NAEYC code of ethical conduct and statement of commitment.* Available at www.naeyc.org/files/naeyc/file/positions/Ethics%20Position%20Statement2011.pdf

Nieto, S. (2012). Honoring the lives of all children: Identity, culture, and language. In B. Falk (Ed.), *Defending childhood: Keeping the promise of early education* (pp. 48–62). New York, NY: Teachers College Press.

Noddings, N. (2005). *The challenge to care in schools* (2nd ed.). New York, NY: Teachers College Press.

Novak, M. (2000). Defining social justice. *First Things* (108), 11–13.

Palmer, P. (2007). *The courage to teach.* Boston, MA: Jossey-Bass.

Passow, A. H., & Elliott, D. L. (1968). The nature and needs of the educationally disadvantaged. In A. H. Passow (Ed.), *Developing programs for the educationally disadvantaged* (pp. 3–19). New York, NY: Teachers College Press.

Peceny, K. (2011). Effective strategies for transitioning bilingual students into mainstream classrooms. *Illinois Reading Council Journal, 39*(1), 20–21.

Pelo, A., & Davidson, F. (2000). *That's not fair: A teacher's guide to activism for young children*. St. Paul, MN: Redleaf Press.

Perry, T., & Fraser, J. W. (1993). *Freedom's plow: Teaching in the multicultural classroom*. New York, NY: Routledge.

Pollard, R. (2011). Ethics in practice: A critical appreciation of Mikhail Bakhtin's concept of "outsidedness" in relation to responsibility and the creating of meaning in psychotherapy. *American Journal of Psychotherapy, 65*(1), 1–25.

Postman, N., & Weingartner, C. (1969). *Teaching as a subversive activity*. New York, NY: Delacorte.

Purpel, D. E. (1989). *The moral and spiritual crisis in education: A curriculum for justice and compassion in education*. New York, NY: Bergen & Garvey.

Purpel, D. E. (2005). *Moral outrage in education*. New York, NY: Peter Lang.

Rawls, J. (1971). *A theory of justice*. Cambridge, MA: Harvard University Press.

Rawls, J. (2001). *Justice as fairness: A restatement*. Cambridge, MA: Belknap Press of Harvard University Press.

Richards, R. (2011). Not in my image: Personalisation and ethnic diversity in the classroom. In G. Richards & F. Armstrong (Eds.), *Teaching and learning in diverse classrooms* (pp. 65–75). London, UK: Routledge.

Robinson, A., & Stark, D. R. (2005). *Advocates in action: Making a difference for young children*. Washington, DC: National Association for the Education of Young Children.

Rothstein, R. (2004). *Class and schools: Using social, economic, and educational reform to close the black–white achievement gap*. New York, NY: Economic Policy Institute and Teachers College.

Ryan, S., & Grieshaber, S. (2004). It's more than child development: Critical theories, research, and teaching young children. *Young Children* (59), 44–92.

Schniedewind, N., & Davidson, E. (1998). *Open minds to equality: A sourcebook of learning activities to affirm diversity and promote equity* (2nd ed.). Boston, MA: Allyn & Bacon.

Searle, J. R. (1969). *Speech acts: An essay in the philosophy of language*. Cambridge, UK: Cambridge University Press.

Sensoy, O., & DiAngelo, R. (2011). *Is everyone equal? An introduction to key concepts in social justice education*. New York, NY: Teachers College Press.

Shetterly, R. (2005). *Americans who tell the truth*. New York, NY: Dutton.

Sockett, H. (1993). *The moral base of teacher professionalism*. New York, NY: Teachers College Press.

Strike, K. A., & Soltis, J. E. (2004). *The ethics of teaching* (4th ed.). New York, NY: Teachers College Press.

Swadener, B. B. (2003). "This is what democracy looks like": Strengthening advocacy in neoliberal times. *Journal of Early Childhood Teacher Education, 24*(1), 135–141.

Taggart, G. (2011). Don't we care? The ethics and emotional labour of early years professionalism. *Early Years, 31*(1), 85–95.

Teaching Tolerance Project. (1997). *Starting small: Teaching tolerance in preschool and early grades*. Montgomery, AL: Southern Poverty Law Center.

Thomas, S. (2011). Teachers and public engagement: An argument for rethinking teacher professionalism to challenge deficit discourses in the public sphere. *Discourse Studies in the Cultural Politics of Education, 32*(3), 371–382.

Thrupp, M., & Tomlinson, S. (2005). Introduction: Education policy, social justice, and "complex hope." *British Education Research Journal, 31*(5), 549–566.

UNICEF. (2013). Convention on the rights of the child. Available at www.unicef.org/crc

U.S. Census Bureau. (2010). Overview of race and Hispanic origin: 2010 Census briefs. Available at www.census.gov/prod/cen2010/briefs/c2010br-02.pdf

Varenne, H., & McDermott, R. (1998). *Successful failure: The schools that America builds*. Boulder, CO: Westview Press.

Warren, S., & Webb, S. (2007). Challenging lifelong learning policy discourse: Where is structure and agency in narrative-based research? *Studies in the Education of Adults, 39*(1), 5–21.

Wasley, P. (2006). Accreditor of educational schools drops controversial "social justice" language. *Chronicle of Higher Education, 52*(41), A13.

Weigel, D. J., & Martin, S. S. (2006). Early childhood research and practice. *Early Childhood Research Quarterly, 15*(1), 295–317.

Williams, L. (1989). Diverse gifts: Multicultural education in the kindergarten. *Childhood Education, 66*(2), 2–3.

Wilson, R. (2005, December 16). Education schools want to make sure prospective teachers have the right "disposition." *Chronicle of Higher Education*, pp. A8–A10.

Wilson, R. (2006, June 25). News blog: Teacher-education accreditor formally drops social justice education. *Chronicle of Higher Education*, pp. A3–A4.

Wollons, R. (Ed.). (1993). *Children at risk in America: History, concepts, and public policy*. Albany, NY: State University of New York Press.

Yoshino, K. (2006). *Covering: The hidden assault on our civil rights*. New York, NY: Random House.

Zajda, J., Majhanovich, S., & Rust, V. (2006). Introduction: Education and social justice. *International Review of Education, 32*(1), 9–22.

Index

About the Author

Beatrice S. Fennimore has focused over 25 years of university teaching, activism, and scholarship on areas related to child advocacy, social policy, public school equity, social justice, and multicultural/anti-bias education. She is a professor of education at Indiana University of Pennsylvania in the Pennsylvania State System of Higher Education, where she teaches a wide range of undergraduate, graduate, and doctoral courses. Dr. Fennimore was a visiting professor at Teachers College, Columbia University, during the 2008–2009 academic year; she also served Teachers College as an adjunct professor for more than 25 years. Among Dr. Fennimore's publications are *Child Advocacy for Early Childhood Educators* and *Talk Matters: Refocusing the Language of Public Schooling* (Teachers College Press), "Know Where You Stand and Stand There" and "Responding to Prejudiced Comments: A Four-Step Method That Works" (*Childhood Education*), "Equity Is Not an Option in Public Education" (*Educational Leadership*), and "Brown and the Failure of Civic Responsibility" (*Teachers College Record*). Dr. Fennimore recently co-edited, with Dr. A. Lin Goodwin, *Promoting Social Justice for Young Children* (2011).